Word Definitions

by Don Roberts

NOVEMBER 1988
Published by
GOSPEL TRACT PUBLICATIONS
411 Hillington Road, Glasgow G52 4BL, Scotland

ISBN 0 948417 37 4
Copyright ©
GOSPEL TRACT PUBLICATIONS

Printed by
GOSPEL TRACT PUBLICATIONS
411 Hillington Road, Glasgow G52 4BL, Scotland

Contents

	Page		Page
Preface	5	Faith	31
Assurance	7	Faithfulness	33
(First mention)		Fasting	34
Assurance	9	Fear of God	35
(Meaning and use)		Fellowship	36
Atonement	11	Firstborn	38
Baptism	12	Flesh	39
Blessing	13	Forgiveness	40
Blood	14	Gift	41
Cleansing	15	Glory	42
Condemnation	16	Gospel	43
Confession	17	Grace	45
Conscience	19	Guilt	47
Conversion	20	Heart	49
Conviction	21	Heaven	50
Cross	22	Hell	51
Death (Eternal)	23	Holy	53
Defilement	25	Hope	54
Deliverance	26	Humility	56
Disobedience	27	Iniquity	58
Election	28	Inspiration	59
Error	29	Jealousy	60
Eternal and		Joy	62
Everlasting	33	Judgment	63

WORD DEFINITIONS

	Page		Page
Justification	65	Repentance	114
Kingdom	67	Resurrection	115
Knowledge	69	Righteousness	116
Law	70	Salvation	118
Liberty	72	Sanctification	121
Life (Eternal)	73	Sanctification	123
Light	74	(Its course through the OT and NT)	
Love	76		
Meditation	78		
Memorial	79	Separation	128
Mercy	81	Sin	129
Miracle	82	Teach	131
Mystery	84	Temptation	133
Name	86	Tidings	135
Obedience	87	Transgression	136
Parable	89	Trespass	138
Pardon	90	Trial	139
Peace	92	Trust	140
Perish	93	Truth	142
Power	94	Ungodliness	144
Praise	96	Unity	145
Prayer	98	Victory	147
Priest	100	Vision	148
Promise	102	Voice	150
Prophecy	103	Washing	151
Propitiation	105	Will of God	153
Ransom	107	The Will of God	154
Reconciliation	108	Works	157
Redemption	110	World	159
Regeneration	111	Worship	161
Remission	113	Wrath	163

Preface

In the light of so much ignorance concerning spiritual matters, coupled with the progressive corruption and ill-usage of the English language, a need has arisen for such a book as this.

It represents the fruit of experience over many years in teaching and preaching the Word of God, where the definition of words and terms has become so necessary. Many such words are taken for granted, and the true meaning (according to Scripture) seldom appreciated.

Each word is treated under three headings:

1. By the law of first mention. i.e. its fundamental meaning is laid down by its first occurrence in Scripture. This principle is used by Paul in Romans 4, citing the case of Abraham who believed God and it was counted unto him for righteousness. It also occurs in Hebrews to explain the priesthood, citing the case of Melchizedek.
2. By comparing the word with its synonyms. i.e. similar words with which it can be confused.
3. By illustrations from Scripture so that the Bible becomes its own commentary, and thereby boasts its own built in lexicon.

I do trust that this book may be a blessing to teacher and preacher alike.

Assurance

First mention
Leviticus 27:19 'And if he that sanctifieth the field will in any wise redeem it, then he shall add the fifth part of the money of thy estimation unto it, and it shall be **assured** him.'

Here, assurance is linked with the redemption of property and the cost involved. It follows redemption—it is the result of redemption.

Synonyms
The word 'assurance' is closely linked with the word 'confidence'. Romans 10:17 teaches that confidence in the Word of God (i.e. taking God at His Word) produces faith. Romans 5:1 teaches that the faith produced results in justification, and I have peace with God, thus giving assurance.

Illustrations from the Scriptures
1 John is associated with knowledge by experience, and first emphasises the assurance of knowing God—EVERYTHING HINGES ON THIS. Every reference given below contains the word 'know':

2:3 Keeping His commandments
 —Practising the Word

2:5 Keeping His Word
    —Practising the Word
2:18 Fulfilment of prophecy. The last time
    —Prophecy in the Word
2:29 Practising righteousness. The family likeness
    —Progress in the spiritual life
3:2 Seeing Him as He is
    —Prospect of His return
3:14 Loving the brethren
    —Product of the spiritual life
3:16 Laid down His life for us
    —Price at Calvary
3:19 Loving in deed and truth
    —Purity of life
3:24 By the Spirit which He hath given us
    —Power of the Spirit
4:2 Jesus Christ come in the flesh
    —Perception
4:6 Spirit of truth, spirit of error
    —Perception
4:13 Given us of His Spirit
    —Promise of His Spirit
5:2 Love God, and keep His commandments
    —Practising the Word
5:13 Because of things written to us
    —Precept
5:15 Know that He hears us
    —Prayer.

Summary and Conclusion

Three 'we knows' in 5:18 to 20, stressing three areas that give assurance:

The Word of God

The Work of Christ
The Witness of the Spirit

A separate treatise is also given on the use and the meaning of this important word, tracing the various words that are employed to express assurance.

Assurance

The Meaning and the Use of the Word

Old Testament

First mention Lev. 27:19 'it shall be assured him' in connection with redemption of property and the cost involved.

Hebrew word is QUM = 'to arise' in Dan. 3:24 'to come forth', 'to exist' in Dan. 2:39. Also 'to stand, endure, remain' in Dan. 2:44. Also 'to establish' in Dan. 6:8. The word was essentially a Chaldean word.

q.v. opposite in Gen. 3:1 'Yea, hath God said' doubting God's word. Satan uses only the word 'God' and not 'Lord God'. LORD = 'Jehovah'. 'Every tree' Satan is devious. Thus assurance is assured by confidence in the Word of God.

q.v. Isa. 32:17 'effects of righteousness—quietness and assurance for ever.' q.v. Rom. 5:1 and peace with God.

Summary so far

Assurance by confidence in the Word of God and related to redemption and the cost involved.

New Testament
Greek words used

peithō = I convince, persuade.

pistis = faith or guarantee. q.v. Acts 17:31 with respect to the resurrection of Christ.

plērophoria = *plēros* (full) + *pherō* (I carry) = full carrying. Full assurance, entire confidence. **Col. 2:2** 'hearts comforted, knit together in love, riches of **full assurance** of understanding. **1 Thess. 1:5** 'gospel in much power, in the Holy Ghost, in **much assurance** 'linked with power and the Holy Spirit. **Heb. 6:11** re. expectation of fulfilment of God's promises. **Heb. 10:22** re. character of faith by which we are to draw near to God.

hupostasis = *hupo* (under) + *histemi* (stand) = standing under. **Heb. 11:1** substance = reality. **q.v. Romans ch.5**.

Remember Assurance is NOT based on feelings, but on facts. A similar 'feeling' can be produced by inhaling laughing gas. Facts are divorced from feelings.

Fruits of Salvation vv.1 to 5   **—LOOKING IN**
Foundation of Salvation vv.6 to 11

          —LOOKING UP

(we have to look up, not down for our foundation. We have the only anchor that goes upward!)

Facts of Salvation vv.12 to 21

          —LOOKING AROUND

Our assurance depends on facts, NOT feelings.

a. **Two Adams** v.14c 'figure of Him to come'
b. **Two Amounts** vv.15,16 'one' and 'many'
c. **Two Authorities** v.17 'death' and 'life'

d. **Two Acts** v.18 'offence' and 'righteousness'
e. **Two Attitudes** v.19 'disobedience' and 'obedience'.

Atonement

First mention

Exodus 29:33 'And they shall eat those things wherewith the **atonement** was made, to consecrate and to sanctify them'.

Atonement is linked with consecration and sanctification and in Leviticus 16:27 the shedding of blood is necessary for atonement.

The Hebrew word first occurs in Genesis 6:14 under the guise of the word 'pitch' and it means 'to cover'.

This word essentially belongs to the Old Testament. The sins of the people were covered, and we are reminded in Hebrews 10:4 'For it is not possible that the blood of bulls and of goats should take away sins'. Thus in Romans 3:25 we read, 'to declare His righteousness for the remission of sins that are past, through the forebearance of God'. So the judgment of past sins was held in suspension until Christ came, 'for nobler blood has flowed from richer veins'. The faith of the Old Testament saints looked forward and our faith looks backwards to the cross of Christ which stands in the centre of the history of men as a monument to the grace of God.

Synonyms

Expiate means to make clear by an act of piety, and is a specific term, whilst 'atone' is a general word. Offences of man to God require an expiatory sacrifice (i.e. the death of the sinless Saviour) to make atonement for all who will accept God's offer of mercy.

Illustrations from Scripture

The parable of the Pharisee and the Publican of Luke 18 shows that the Publican in begging for mercy, was asking God to take away the guilt of his sin. This could only be done through the shedding of the blood of Christ.

Baptism

First mention

Matthew 3:6 'And were **baptized** of him in Jordan, confessing their sins'.

Baptism, here, is linked with water, the preposition 'in', and confessing of sins.

Baptism is immersion —death
　　　　　　submersion —burial
　　　　　　emergence —resurrection.

The Acts of the Apostles employs the phrase 'repent and be baptized' in one breath. The two are linked. Baptism is NOT salvation, but is complimentary to it.

Synonyms

Both Confirmation (admitting to full communion) and Christening (a sprinkling at birth) are foreign to the teaching of Scripture. Baptism is for believers only and follows repentance.

Illustrations from the Scriptures
1 Corinthians 10:2 talks of the people of God baptized unto Moses in the cloud and in the sea. This was the experience of a redeemed people, having left Egypt behind. It expressed their loyalty and allegiance to their leader Moses, the mediator of the old covenant. So we, as baptized believers, a redeemed people, give our loyalty and allegiance to the Leader of the new covenant, the Lord Jesus Christ, better than Moses (Hebrews 3).

Blessing

First mention
Genesis 1:22 'And God **blessed** them, saying, Be fruitful, and multiply, and fill the waters in the seas, and let fowl multiply in the earth'. Whilst this verse is concerned with animals, the principle is still the same—blessing is linked with reproduction and growth. Genesis 12:2 talks of blessing for Abraham, and is linked with obedience to God's commandments.

Synonyms
Happiness is that which is adapted to our present condition and admits of degrees, since every individual is placed in different circumstances, which fit him to be more or less happy. Blessing is that which is purely spiritual, and rises above the ordinary level of human enjoyments.

Illustrations from the Scriptures
Jacob's experience recorded in Genesis 32:24 to 32,

shows that the blessing he sought with tears, was on a higher plane than the material blessings he enjoyed. A careful re-examination of this passage will reveal what blessing really is. The road to blessing was a lonely path for Jacob, and was nothing short of a struggle with tears. 'I will not let Thee go' is the passport for blessing and Jacob persisted—he had not wrestled all night for nothing!

Blood

First mention
Genesis 4:10 'the voice of thy brother's **blood** crieth unto me from the ground' This verse teaches (albeit human blood) that it has a voice. Heb 12:24 'And to Jesus the mediator of the new covenant, and to the blood of sprinkling, that speaketh better things than that of Abel'.

Synonyms
Both life and death are implied in the word 'blood'. Leviticus 17:11 'For the life of the flesh is in the blood'. But when reference is made to the blood of Christ, it means death applied. It obviously refers to the cross of Christ, and it represents God's side of the cross. Exodus 12:13 'when I see the blood, I will passover you'.

Illustrations from the Scriptures
The benefits and the results of the blood of Christ are to be learnt from the Old Testament types. There were three applications of the blood. It could be put, poured, or sprinkled. When it was sprinkled the finger pointed to the mercy seat.

In Leviticus 16 the high priest only enters the holy place **with blood**.

In Exodus, redemption was first by blood, and then by power. After Exodus 12 they were a redeemed people, never to return to Egypt again. The killing of the passover lamb, and the application of the blood was not a priestly function, for there was no priesthood at that time. The priesthood did not appear till after Exodus 24, when Moses came down from the mount with the pattern of the tabernacle. It was the responsibility of each household to take the lamb and to apply the blood.

Cleansing

First mention
Exodus 29:36 'And thou shalt offer every day a bullock for a sin offering for atonement; and thou shalt **cleanse** the altar, when thou hast made an atonement for it, and thou shalt anoint it, to sanctify it'.

Cleansing is linked with atonement and sanctification and holiness.

Synonyms
Wash implies an ablution employing water. Washing and cleansing use two different agents. Washing with blood is an expression foreign to the law, and conveys an idea which seems at variance with its teaching. Revelation 1:5 is better translated 'loosed us from our sins', rather than 'washed us from our sins'.

Illustrations from the Scriptures
In Leviticus 13 and the cleansing of the leper, he was

pronounced clean when the leprosy had covered all his flesh (verse 13). This seems a grave contradiction except for the fact that if leprosy turned inward, then was the leper pronounced unclean. The leprosy in turning outward is a type of the sinner confessing his sins. He may not have felt clean, but he was clean. So the sinner may not feel saved, but he is according to the Word of God.

Condemnation

First mention

Exodus 22:9 'For all manner of trespass, whether it be for ox, for ass, for sheep, for raiment, or for any manner of lost thing, which another challengeth to be his, the cause of both parties shall come before the judges; and whom the judges shall **condemn**, he shall pay double unto his neighbour'.

Notice how the sentence pronounced is differentiated from the sentence executed. These are legal terms. The condemning of the judges was the sentence pronounced, whilst the actual paying of the double portion is the sentence executed to satisfy the law.

Synonyms

Apparently similar words are: blame, reprove, reproach, upbraid, and censure.

Reproach and upbraid are the acts of an equal, whilst blame, reprove and condemn are the acts of a superior. Thus masters blame or reprove their servants, whilst friends and acquaintances reproach and upbraid each other.

Blame, reproof, and upbraiding are always addressed directly to the individual person, whilst reproach, censure, and condemnation, are often conveyed through an indirect channel. Blame, reproach, upbraid, and condemn, may be applied to ourselves, whilst reproof and censure are applied to others. We blame ourselves for acts of imprudence; our consciences reproach us for our weaknesses, and we are condemned for our sins.

Illustrations from the Scriptures
In John 3:18, the word must be sharply defined when preaching the gospel, or confusion will result. The casual reader will think that there is no hope for his soul. He is already condemned, so why bother? He has closed his mind, and he is not listening to the preacher anymore. Differentiate between condemnation (the sentence pronounced) and punishment (the sentence executed). In the forensic world there is a time interval between the sentence pronounced, and the sentence executed. That is the day of grace, the day of opportunity. Now make your point. It is not reprieve that God offers, it is pardon, yea, more than pardon, it is justification by grace; and that means the sinner is declared not guilty, and he does not even deserve it. Careful study of the epistle of Romans is necessary to grasp this great truth.

Confession

First mention
Leviticus 5:5 'And it shall be, when he shall be guilty of one of these things, that he shall **confess** that he hath

sinned in that thing'. The word is inseparably linked with sin and the guilt that it produces. In verse 6 confession is closely followed by atonement and the attendant shedding of blood.

Synonyms

Acknowledging is a simple declaration, whilst confessing and owning are private communications, and avowal is a public declaration. Thus we acknowledge facts, confess our faults and sins, and avow motives and opinions.

We acknowledge in consequence of a charge, and we avow voluntarily.

We acknowledge having been concerned in a transaction; we confess our guilt; we own that a thing is wrong; but we are ashamed to avow our motives.

Candour leads to an acknowledgement; repentance produces a confession; the desire of forgiveness leads to owning.

Illustrations from the Scriptures

1 John 1:9 deals with confession, and 1 John 2:1 deals with advocacy. Under the Old Testament types, they are linked with washing and the priesthood respectively. The first has to do with the Father's house, and the other with 'the house of God' (i.e. the sanctuary). Christ is 'a Son over His own house' Hebrews 3:6, and He is also 'an high priest over the house of God'. We are the household of the Son, and we have access to the house of God.

Conscience

First mention
John 8:9 'And they which heard it, being convicted by their own **conscience**, went out one by one, beginning at the eldest, even unto the last: and Jesus was left alone, and the woman standing in the midst'.

The word is linked with sin, guilt and conviction in the context, and brought about a positive reaction—they left the scene. They were not asked to leave, but they did so at their own peril. The woman remained there and heard words whereby she might be saved.

Synonyms
Conscience to scruples is as the whole to a part. Scruples concern particular things, even trifling or minor points. Conscience concerns weightier matters, even the whole man, and his way of life.

Illustrations from the Scriptures
Hebrews 10:22 refers to 'an evil conscience'. This seems to suggest that such a conscience acts in the opposite way to a good or pure conscience. It approves the wrong and disapproves the right. Such is the effect in a man who never listens to his conscience.

Pain in the body, although unpleasant, can be a blessing, because it tells us when something is wrong. So the conscience is a pain in the soul that cannot correct the error, but tells us that something is wrong.

Conversion

First mention

Psalm 19:7 'The law of the LORD is perfect, **converting** the soul: the testimony of the LORD is sure, making wise the simple'.

Conversion concerns the soul, implies a complete change, and is in antiphase to the world's philosophy on life—it makes wise the simple.

Synonyms

In secular terms, conversion only means a change from one standard to another i.e. 32°F converted to centigrade is 0°C—no change in the temperature, only a change in standard. Convert is more extensive in its sense and application than proselyte. Convert in its full sense includes every change of opinion and direction, for salvation is a change in every sense, and in every department of the life. Proselyte in its strict sense refers only to change from one religious belief to another.

Conversion is a more voluntary act than proselytism. Conversion is an inward change, whilst proselytism is an outward change.

The conversion of the sinner is the work of God's grace, and it is an act of great presumption, therefore, in those men who rest so strongly on their own particular modes and forms in bringing about this great work. Thus the proselyte is often the creature and tool of a party.

When a sinner realises that conversion is a change of direction, he realises that the things of God are diametrically opposed to the things of this world.

Illustrations from the Scriptures

In Genesis, before the fall, man had a face that looked upwards to God, and this was the normal condition. But sin brought estrangement; and our race springs, not from Adam in his innocence before the fall, but from the fallen outcast. By nature man's face is now averted from his God (man's natural condition is now abnormal). He needs, therefore, to be turned right around again—and that is conversion.

Conviction

First mention

Job 32:12 'Yea, I attended unto you, and, behold, there was none of you that convinced (**convicted**) Job, or that answered his words'.

Here the lack of conviction is because of the lack of evidence.

In John 8:9 conviction is linked with the conscience and the guilt of sin.

Synonyms

What convinces binds; what persuades attracts. We are convinced or convicted by arguments; we are persuaded by entreaties and personal influence. We are convinced that a thing is true or false; we are easily persuaded to do that which favours our own interests. Conviction respects our most important duties; persuasion is applied to matters of indifference.

The first step to true repentance is a thorough conviction of the enormity of sin. As conviction is the effect of substantial evidence, it is solid and permanent in its nature; it cannot be so easily changed and deceived. Persuasion, depending upon our feelings, is influenced by external objects, and exposed to various changes. Conviction answers in our minds to positive certainty; persuasion answers to probability.

Illustrations from the Scriptures

John 16:8 to 11. Man's probation is at an end. The Holy Spirit has come, not to re-open the question of sin, righteousness and judgment, but to convince the world that it is closed for ever. He convicts of sin, because the Son of God has been cast out by the world; righteousness because the Outcast of the world has been welcomed by the Father in heaven; and judgment, because Satan, the architect of Christ's rejection, has now himself been judged.

Cross

First mention

Matthew 10:38 'And he that taketh not his **cross**, and followeth after me, is not worthy of me'. 'His cross' does not imply that everyone has their own cross. It is the cross of Christ, and it becomes ours by identification.

The cross of Christ implies following Him, and allegiance and loyalty to Him.

The poet, Robert Browning, gives his own definition of a woman: 'last at the cross, and first at the grave'.

Synonyms

The term 'the death of Christ' and the term 'the cross of

Christ' mean the same things. It is not that God separates them, but man does. The term 'the death of Christ' leaves the self respect of man intact, it does not hurt his pride. It will give no offence to anyone, nor be branded as foolishness. But the preaching of the cross shows man as he really is—a naked sinner trembling on the brink of hell.

Illustrations from the Scriptures
The epistle to the Galatians displays the cross prominently to refute the errors of retrogressive bondage and a return to the things of the flesh, as taught by the Judaizing teachers.

Chapter 2 and verse 20 means that my old self (as well as the world in chapter 6 and verse 14) must wither and die on the cross. It is the reproduction of the cross in me. The way that Paul preached the cross is given to us in chapter 3 and verse 1. 'Evidently set forth before their eyes' is the imagery of a large display, a placard that would immediately catch the eye.

Death (eternal)

First mention
Genesis 2:17 'But of the tree of the knowledge of good and evil, thou shalt not eat of it: for in the day that thou eatest thereof thou shalt surely **die**'. This verse should be coupled with verses 3 and 4 of the next chapter. In one sense they did die, and in one sense they did not die. The serpent did not define what he meant by dying. They died spiritually, but they did not die (at that time)

physically. Death here is linked with disobedience to the commandment of God.

Synonyms

There is physical death, there is spiritual death, and there is eternal death. But what is the common link? Physical death can be described as:

departure—a passage from one life to another.

decease—a legal term, involving the leaving of property to survivors.

demise—a regal term, implying a laying down and resigning of possessions.

For the believer physical death is an arrival rather than a departure (2 Peter 1:11).

Illustrations from the Scriptures

To answer my question, Luke chapter 15 supplies the answer. If we can understand how a prodigal son could be dead and alive at the same time, we have found the answer. To the father the son was dead because he was separated from the father. And so it is with man. Death brings alienation and separation from God. Thus a man can be dead and alive at the same time. Surely this last verse in chapter 15 paves the way for chapter 16 and the bliss of Lazarus and the woe of the rich man. This rich man was alive in as much as he could speak, see, feel, and recognise; yet he was dead, eternally dead—separated from God. Man fixes the gulfs in this life, but God fixes the gulf in eternity.

Defilement

First mention
Genesis 34:2 'And when Shechem the son of Hamor the Hivite, prince of the country, saw her, he took her, and lay with her, and **defiled** her.'

Defilement concerns the flesh and self will, and is the product of sin. The man's action not only defiled himself, but the woman also.

Synonyms
Degrade concerns the external rank or station.
Disgrace refers to the moral estimation or character.
Defile refers to internal pollution and corruption.
The higher the rank of the individual, the greater his degradation; the higher his character, or the more sacred his office, the greater his disgrace.
Defilement knows no rank or office—it is the fruit of universal sin.

Illustrations from the Scriptures
Exodus, in its types, teaches redemption by blood and by power, in that order. The epistle of Romans takes up the theme in terms of justification and sanctification. Romans chapters 3, 4 and 5 teach justification by grace, faith and blood—thus taking away the guilt of our sins on the ground of grace, by faith, and through the instrumentality of the blood of Christ. Romans 6, 7, and 8 teach sanctification in terms of being dead to sin, dead to the law, and dead to the flesh; thus removing the defilement of sin.

To summarize: sin produces
- guilt —hence the need for justification
- defilement —hence the need for sanctification
- estrangement—hence the need for reconciliation.

Deliverance

First mention
Genesis 45:7 'And God sent me before you to preserve you a posterity in the earth, and to save your lives by a great **deliverance**.'

This verse teaches that deliverance is God's initiative, and involves life and salvation, together with preservation and posterity.

Synonyms
The idea of taking or keeping from danger is common to the three terms, deliver, rescue and save. Deliver and rescue signify rather to take from danger, and save to keep from danger. We are delivered and rescued from present evil whilst we are saved from evil yet to come.

A person may be delivered from a burden, from an oppression, from a disease, or from danger. A prisoner is rescued from the hands of an enemy. A person is saved from destruction.

Illustrations from the Scriptures
In the early chapters of Exodus the immediate problem was deliverance from the bondage and slavery of Egypt. To work out their destiny was impossible until they had been delivered from slavery; and that deliverance was impossible save by the power of God.

We learn from the typology of Exodus, that the Passover and its attendant deliverance for the people of God, was but the first step in the full salvation of the people.

Disobedience

First mention
1 Kings 13:21 'And he cried unto the man of God that came from Judah, saying, Thus saith the LORD, Forasmuch as thou hast **disobeyed** the mouth of the LORD, and hast not kept the commandment which the LORD thy God commanded thee.'

The word is closely connected with listening to and carrying out the commandments of God, or rather the lack of doing so, with the attendant danger of judgment.

Synonyms
There is disobedience to a command, but lack of submission to power, or the will of God. Disobedience destroys life and unity, and implies a refusal to hear.

We may be disobedient to the command of a person, but disrespectful to the person giving the command.

Illustrations from the Scriptures
Matthew 21:28 to 31 portrays two sons; one was obedient, and the other was disobedient. The last mentioned son was most polite—'I go, sir' but was disobedient. The first son was rude—'I will not' and repented and became obedient. There are many rebellious believers who have repented and are now doing the will of the Father.

Election

First mention

Isaiah 42:1 'Behold my servant, whom I uphold; mine **elect**, in whom my soul delighteth; I have put my spirit upon him: he shall bring forth judgment to the Gentiles'.

Election, here, stresses the purposes of God, the will of God, and His delight.

Synonyms

The two terms 'choose' and 'elect' are employed in regard to persons appointed to an office; the former in a general sense, the latter in a particular sense.

People are obliged to serve in some offices when they are chosen. The circumstances of being elected are an honour after which they eagerly aspire; and for the attainment of which they risk their property, and use the most strenuous exertions.

Election suggests picking out and selecting. That which is picked and selected is always the best of its kind. Soldiers are sometimes picked to form a particular regiment. Pieces are selected in prose or verse for general purposes.

Illustrations from the Scriptures

2 Thessalonians 2:13 states that we have been chosen to salvation from the beginning and the means was the preaching of the gospel. Let us be careful how we preach the gospel in the light of the truth of election. By all means bring salvation within the reach of the sinner, but not to make him independent of God. On the other hand if a sinner be elect, God is bound to save him; and

that if he be not elect, God cannot save him. Remember that election depends on the sovereignty of God.

The gospel is not like a magnet with power over only the elect. Forgiveness may be preached to all because all may share it. God beseeches men to be reconciled, because He has provided a reconciliation. Election cannot limit the value of the death of Christ.

Error

First mention
Leviticus 5:18 'And he shall bring a ram without blemish out of the flock, with thy estimation, for a trespass offering, unto the priest: and the priest shall make an atonement for him concerning his ignorance wherein he **erred** and wist it not, and it shall be forgiven him.'

Error is linked with ignorance here, and therefore the need for teaching.

Synonyms
Error is the lot of man, and into whatever we attempt to do or think, error will be sure to creep. The term therefore is unlimited in its use and the very mention of it reminds us of our condition. We experience errors of judgment, errors of calculation and errors of the heart. Other terms only denote modes of error.

A mistake is an error of choice. Blunder is an error of action.

A mistake must be rectified, and a blunder must be set right. But an error must be counteracted by positive truth, for error is not only the opposite to truth, but is directly opposed to it.

Illustrations from the Scriptures

Psalm 14:1 states 'the fool hath said in his heart, There is no God'. He says it in his heart—he whispers it to himself in secret. There is no darkness like that which covers us when a strong light is quenched.

The problem with the believers addressed in the epistle to the Hebrews, was their ignorance of the basic truths of the function of the priesthood. Chapter 5 verse 12 states: 'For when for the time ye ought to be teachers, ye have need that one teach you again which be the first principles of the oracles of God; and are become such as have need of milk, and not of strong meat'.

Eternal and Everlasting

First mention (everlasting)

Genesis 9:16 'And the bow shall be in the cloud; and I will look upon it, that I may remember the **everlasting** covenant between God and every living creature of all flesh that is upon the earth'.

First mention (eternal)

Deuteronomy 33:27 'The **eternal** God is thy refuge, and underneath are the **everlasting** arms: and he shall thrust out the enemy from before thee; and shall say, Destroy them.'

The word 'eternal' relates to the Being and character of God, and the word 'everlasting' refers to God's actions and their consequences.

Synonyms

The eternal is set above time, whilst the endless lies within time. Endless has beginning and no end. Eternal has neither beginning nor end. God is therefore eternal. There is an eternal state of bliss or misery according to one's attitude to Christ; but their joys or sorrows may be endless as regards to this life.

That which is endless has no cessation; that which is everlasting has neither interruption nor cessation.

Endless is used of existing things. The everlasting extends into futurity. Hence we speak of endless disputes, and endless warfare; but an everlasting memorial, and an everlasting crown.

Illustrations from the Scriptures

Luke chapter 16 draws the curtain to one side and gives us a glimpse into eternity. The scene yields some important clues to the meaning of our words. Despite the pleas of the rich man in hell, Lazarus could not leave the bosom of Abraham for one second to tend to this former superior. The bliss that heaven yields is uninterrupted. Also the misery that the rich man experienced was not alleviated for one second.

Faith

First mention

Genesis 15:6 'And he **believed** in the LORD; and he counted it to him for righteousness'. This is quoted by Paul in Romans chapter 4 when dealing with the great gospel truth of justification by faith. The fundamental truth behind the meaning of faith is taking God at His word, and confidence in that word. This concept is outlined in Romans 10:17 'So then faith cometh by hearing, and hearing by the word of God'.

Synonyms

To define faith by the word 'trust' is to substitute a word that needs defining for the word one is endeavouring to define. It is an endless circle. Saving faith is taking God at His word, as we have already said; but trust etymologically is linked with hope. Let us put the two words to the test. Ephesians 2:8 'For by grace are ye saved through trust'. Oh no! says the bible scholar, the word should be faith—then there **is** a difference between the two words. Trust springs from confidence in the person trusted; and that depends on knowledge of the person confided in or believed in. As the years go by we learn to trust the Lord simply because we know Him better.

Faith denotes a way of life, whilst fidelity is a disposition of the mind to adhere to that faith. We keep our faith, whilst we show our fidelity.

Faith depends on promises, whilst fidelity depends upon relationships and connections.

No treaty can be made with him who will keep no faith, whilst no confidence can be placed in him who discovers no fidelity.

Belief and credit are particular actions, whilst faith and trust are permanent dispositions of the mind and heart.

Faith has always to do with the heart and mind, whilst creed only respects the thing which is the object of faith.

Illustrations from the Scriptures

Hebrews 11:1 is not so much a definition of faith, but the sphere and product of faith.

It is by faith that: we are wise v.3
we worship v.4
we walk v.5
we work v.7.

The parable of the Pharisee and the Publican in Luke 18 yields some important information about faith. Because the publican went down to his house justified, faith is the means by which we receive from God, not give to Him. The Pharisee had every thing to give; the Publican had nothing to give. The Pharisee came to be seen; the Publican came to be heard.

Romans 4:16 teaches us that faith is not merit—'Therefore it is of faith, that it might be by grace'.

Seeing is believing says the world. No! believing is seeing. See John 9.

The world declares that it must understand before it can believe. No! Hebrews 11:2 teaches that it is by faith that we understand.

Some think that they must pray for faith. But we need faith to pray!

Faithfulness

First mention

Numbers 12:7 'My servant Moses is not so, who is **faithful** in all mine house'.

The word is used here in connection with God's house

and the transmission of God's message. The verse reappears in Hebrews 3 verses 2 and 5, set in contrast to Christ who is counted worthy of more glory than Moses. From Hebrews we learn that faithfulness and the servant are closely linked.

Synonyms

It is the duty of the believer to be faithful to all his engagements; it is a particular quality in a servant to be trusty. Trusty may be applied equally to persons or things. We may speak of a faithful saying, or a faithful picture; we may also speak of a trusty sword, or a trusty weapon.

Illustrations from the Scriptures

Luke 16 leaves on record the parable of the unjust steward, which leads up to the episode concerning the rich man and Lazarus, and it give us some important clues to the meaning of faithfulness.

The steward was like the rich man in being unfaithful in the things that God had entrusted to him. He could not be responsible for his own things, if he could not be responsible for that which was another's. Verse 18 is by no means out of context when it deals with divorce, because the problem is unfaithfulness.

Fasting

First mention

Judges 20:26 'Then all the children of Israel, and all the people, went up, and came unto the house of God, and wept, and sat there before the Lord, and **fasted** that day until evening, and offered burnt offerings and peace offerings before the LORD.'

Fasting is connected with prayer, and it is before the Lord. The request of the children of Israel with respect to a victory over the tribe of Benjamin was becoming a problem, because the people had been defeated. The third request was accomplished with fasting and tears, and victory was realised.

Synonyms
Abstinence is a general term, applicable to any object from which we abstain. Fast is a species of abstinence, namely an abstaining from food. Such fasting is usually linked with prayer. It is not a thing that one would talk about—it is done before the Lord.

Illustrations from the Scriptures
2 Samuel 12 portrays the concern of David for the first child that Bathsheba gave him. To fast and pray while the child was still alive was right, but to fast and pray for the child after the death of the child was too late.

Matthew 6:17 and 18 teaches us to behave normally when we fast and to do it in secret as before the Lord.

Fear of God

First mention
Genesis 20:11 'And Abraham said, Because I thought, Surely the **fear of God** is not in this place; and they will slay me for my wife's sake.'

Here, the reference is a negative one i.e. the absence of

the fear of God, linked with the untimely dread of Abraham.

Genesis 22:12 'And he said, Lay not thine hand upon the lad, neither do thou anything unto him: for now I know that thou **fearest God**, seeing thou hast not withheld thy son, thine only son from me.'

Here, the reference is a positive one i.e. the presence of the fear of God, linked with the willingness of Abraham to give all that he had (in the person of his son, Isaac) to God.

Synonyms
Fear and dread affect the mind, whilst fright, terror, and horror affect the senses.

The thought of death is dreadful to one who feels himself unprepared; whilst a contest is fearful when the issue is important. Dread tends to be negative, whilst fear tends to be positive. The fear of God is like the fear for a parent, in the sense of not wishing to diplease.

Illustrations from the Scriptures
Malachi 3:16 teaches that there is a bond between all that fear the Lord; it is a ground of fellowship. The Lord takes interest in the conversations of such people and it is never forgotten. The fear of the Lord is coupled with thinking upon His name, implying reverence, respect and honour to His name.

Fellowship

First mention
Leviticus 6:2 'If a soul sin, and commit a trespass against the Lord, and lie unto his neighbour in that which was

delivered him to keep, or in **fellowship**, or in a thing taken by violence, or hath deceived his neighbour;'

It is used here in connection with my relationship to my neighbour, and trust and keeping.

The loss of fellowship is because of the works of the flesh i.e. lying, violence, and deception.

Synonyms

Fellowship is said of people as individuals; society of them collectively.

We talk about fellowship with each other, and joining a society.

Association is founded on unity of sentiment as well as unity of object; but it is mostly unorganized, and kept together only by the spirit which gives rise to it.

A society requires nothing but unity of object, which is permanent in its nature.

Companies are brought together for the purposes of interest, and are dissolved when that object ceases to exist.

Partnerships are altogether of an individual and private nature, because they are without organization and system.

Illustrations from the Scriptures

Luke 5 teaches something about fellowship in the fishermen who were partners in their trade. There was fellowship in the menial task of washing the nets. There was fellowship in the sleepless nights when trying to get a catch. There was fellowship in their failures, when they caught nothing. There was fellowship in their successes when the haul was large. Acts 2:42 declares that they continued steadfastly in **the** fellowship. (The definite article is wanting in the A.V. text.) This fellowship was different to all other fellowships. The text of chapter 2 gives us the clue to the meaning of the word. Verse 1—they were **all** with **one accord in one place**. It included everyone; they were in agreement, and there was unity. Verse 44 states that they were **together**, and had all **things common**. There was harmony and sharing. Verse 45 explains how they met each other's needs, whilst verse 46 states that they **continued daily**. This was no 'once a week exercise', but a way of life.

Firstborn

First mention

Genesis 10:15 'And Canaan begat Sidon his **firstborn**, and Heth'. Here the word means simply the first result of the union in marriage.

Genesis 27:19 'And Jacob said unto his father, I am Esau thy **firstborn**; I have done according as thou badest me: arise, I pray thee, sit and eat of my venison, that thy soul may bless me.'

Quite clearly Jacob was not the firstborn in the sense already defined. See further on and the comments on Romans 9.

Synonyms

Firstlings are the results of the herd; whilst firstfruits are the first results of the harvest. Sometimes the terms are interchanged. But, according to Scripture the firstborn is not always the one born first.

Illustrations from the Scriptures
Turning then to Romans 9, more light is shed on Esau and Jacob. Verse 12 states that the elder shall serve the younger, and verse 13 states that Jacob was loved, but Esau was hated. This situation was so **before** not **after** their birth, that it might not be of works. Thus in the case of the firstborn we are talking about privilege.

Flesh

First mention
Genesis 6:3 (in the sense in which we are discussing the word) 'And the LORD said, My spirit shall not always strive with man, for that he also is **flesh**: yet his days shall be an hundred and twenty years'.

The two preceeding references are used in a good sense, but here (more in line with our subject) the word is used in a bad sense, and immediately the striving between the Spirit and the flesh is established, indicating that the things of the flesh are diametrically opposed to the things of God.

Synonyms
Self, sensuality and the like seem to be the products of the generic term 'flesh', a sinister catalogue of which is found in Galatians 5.

Illustrations from the Scriptures
In 1 John 2:16 the lust of the flesh is linked with that which the eye sees, and the exaltation of man. It is all a product of this world which will pass away. Galatians 5

contrasts the works (plural) of the flesh and the fruit (singular) of the Spirit. Verse 17 highlights the constant battle between the Spirit and the flesh, taking us back to the Genesis narrative with which we began.

Forgiveness

First mention

Genesis 50:17 'So shall ye say unto Joseph, Forgive, I pray thee now, the trespass of thy brethren, and their sin; for they did unto thee evil: and now, we pray thee, **forgive** the trespass of the servants of the God of thy father. And Joseph wept when they spake unto him'.

Forgiveness is directly connected with the awareness of wrong doing to a person. It is something to be asked for. It is first a divine quality, but it is also a human quality. There is a profound effect upon the person who is asked to forgive.

Synonyms

God forgives as a Father, but pardons as a judge. Man can forgive but not forget. God can forgive and forget. Or as the Psalmist puts it 'our sins are remembered no more'. This attribute can only be of God.

Pardon of sin obliterates that which is past and restores the sinner. Remission of sin alone averts the Divine vengeance which otherwise would fall upon the guilty.

Illustrations from the Scriptures

Romans 3:25 talks about remission. It is not the word for forgiveness. Forgiveness is the work of grace. Here it is forebearance. The passing over of the former sins were dealt with at the cross. Thus the cross of Christ stands in the centre of the history of mankind.

Those that lived before the cross possessed a faith that looked forward, whilst those that lived after the cross possess a faith that looks backward.

As I said forgiveness is a work of grace—it is undeserved—we have no prior claim on God. The cross of Christ has outraged every claim that man had on God. It has levelled every distinction. The ground in front of the cross is level.

Gift

First mention

Genesis 34:12 'Ask me never so much dowry and **gift**, and I will give according as ye shall say unto me: but give me the damsel to wife.'

Although the incident is not a happy one, we nevertheless see how much a man was willing to give for what he must have.

'For God so loved the world that He gave His only begotten Son'—look at the gift that God gave to win the soul of man.

Synonyms

The gift is an act of generosity or condescension; it contributes to the benefit of the receiver. The present is an act of kindness, courtesy, or respect; it contributes to the pleasure of the receiver. The gift passes from the rich to the poor, from the high to the low, and creates an obligation. The present passes either between equals or from the inferior to the superior. Whatever we receive from God is a gift; whatever we receive from a friend is a present.

The gift is private, and benefits the individual; the donation is public, and serves some general purpose.

Illustrations from the scriptures

Ephesians 2:8 'For by grace are ye saved through faith; and that (salvation) not of yourselves: it is the gift of God'. Salvation is the gift of God because we cannot afford it—the price is too high. It is given on the principle of grace—we do not deserve it. It is received on the principle of faith. In this verse faith is not the gift of God—salvation is the gift of God. Faith cometh by hearing.

Glory

First mention

Exodus 16:7 (with respect to the glory of God, not man) 'And in the morning, then ye shall see the **glory** of the LORD; for that he heareth your murmurings against the LORD: and what are we, that ye murmur against us?'

The glory of the Lord is closely connected with that which the Lord is able to do for His people. Therefore the glory of the Lord is not only appreciated and recognised, but actually seen in what He is able to do.

Synonyms

Glory is connected with extraordinary efforts and to

great undertakings; it is connected with everything which has a peculiar public interest; honour is more properly obtained within a private circle.

Glory is not confined to the nation or life of the individual; it spreads over all the earth. Honour (to God) is limited to those who appreciate His glory, who are witnesses of His mighty acts.

Illustrations from the Scriptures

Romans 1 sheds some light on the meaning of the glory of God. Verses 20 and 21 teach that recognition of the glory of God is related to the power of God in creation, His Godhead, and the knowledge of Him. The glory of God cannot be changed—it is as unchangeable as God Himself is. The idea behind verse 23 is that the glory of God has been EXCHANGED for an image made like to corruptible man. Man, who is corrupt in himself, and is capable of corrupting others.

Gospel

First mention

Matthew 4:23 'And Jesus went about all Galilee teaching in their synagogues, and preaching the **gospel** of the kingdom, and healing all manner of sickness and all manner of disease among the people.'

The gospel is closely linked here with both teaching and preaching. Many think today that the gospel should be both taught and preached. i.e. there is always a word for the believer in the gospel message. The message of the gospel will never cease to thrill the soul of the believer.

It is also linked with the kingdom, and the fact that the Lord did not stay in one place, but moved from place to place, preaching the gospel.

Synonyms

News and tidings are words that are used in place of the word gospel. (Look up the word 'tiding' in this volume). News implies anything new that is circulated, whilst tidings (from tide) signifies that which flows in periodically like the tide. News is unexpected, tidings are expected. In what sense is the gospel described as news? News implies something new, and how can the death of Christ (2,000 years ago) be described as something new? The point is that the word 'news' can also describe something one has never heard or realised before. Therefore it is necessary when preaching the gospel to emphasise that all have sinned, and the need of a Saviour. It is also necessary to emphasise the meaning of such words that this book deals with. These are the things that man is not aware of.

Illustrations from the Scriptures

The epistle to the Romans is the first book to define the gospel of Christ. The key verse is chapter 1:16 and it tells us what the gospel is (the power of God unto salvation), whilst verse 17 relates it to the righteousness of God. The entire book repays careful studying for it defines the following terms covered in this book:

Sin	chs.1 to 3, and in particular 3:23
Remission	3:25
Justification by Grace	ch.3
Justification by Faith	ch.4
Justification by Blood	5:9

Assurance	ch.5
Reconciliation	ch.5
The Love of God	ch.5
Sanctification	chs.6,7 and 8
Adoption	ch.8
Election	ch.9
Faith	ch.10

These are great and mighty truths, indispensable in the teaching and the preaching of the gospel.

The etymology of the word is interesting. One source suggests that the word is derived from the Old English GODSPEL, originally GOOD SPEL = good tidings. The other source suggests that SPEL is derived from the German SPIEL = a story (the German word has lost that meaning now). Therefore the Gospel is God's story of Christ. Not man's story of Christ, but God's. Man's story of Christ would start with His birth and end with His death. God's story of Christ commences in eternity (John 1) through His birth, life, death, resurrection, ascension, His return, and the consummation of the ages. This is the full Gospel of Christ; and we are charged with the responsibility of declaring ALL the counsel of God.

Grace

First mention

Genesis 6:8 'But Noah found **grace** in the eyes of the LORD'.

We learn from this verse that grace has its source in God, not man. God gives by grace, man receives by faith

(Ephesians 2:8). Grace is something that can be found. It is presented in dark contrast to the evil of man. Thus grace is always linked with that which man does not deserve. Man only deserves judgment.

Synonyms

Grace and favour can be easily confused with each other. Grace is never used but in regard to those who have offended and made themselves liable to punishment. Grace results from pure kindness (see Titus 3) independently of merit (if any) of the receiver.

Favour is employed for actual good. An act of grace is employed to denote that act of the government by which insolvent debtors are released. In our context it denotes that merciful influence which God exerts over His most unworthy creatures from the infinite goodness of His Divine nature.

The term favour is employed indiscriminately with regard to man or God. Those who are in power have the greatest opportunity of conferring favours; but all we receive at the hands of God must be acknowledged as a favour.

The grace of God is absolutely indispensable for men as sinners to be saved.

Illustrations from the Scriptures

1 Timothy 1:11 talks of the glorious gospel of the blessed God, or more correctly the gospel of the glory of the blessed God. We must preach grace. If we preach a mixed gospel, and play down, or exclude grace, we are robbing God of His glory.

John 1:17 states that grace came by Jesus Christ, albeit in His humiliation. But grace now reigns supreme. As grace be on the throne, what limits can be imposed upon it? God can bless in spite of what man did to Christ at Calvary. It is not that Calvary has failed to quench the love of God toward men, but Calvary is the proof and measure of that love, as we learn in Romans 5:8.

Grace is conqueror and grace reigns. Not at the expense of righteousness, but in virtue of it.

Grace and mercy are complimentary to each other.

Grace is giving to us that which we do not deserve. God alone being the great giver.

Mercy is holding back (by God) that which we do deserve.

Guilt

First mention

Genesis 26:10 'And Abimelech said, What is this thou hast done unto us? one of the people might lightly have lien with thy wife, and thou shouldest have brought **guiltiness** upon us'.

Guilt here is linked with:
    falsehood—see verse 9
    fear   —'What is this thou hast done to us?'
    flesh   —'lien with thy wife'.

Synonyms

Crime is concerned with the character of the offence, whilst guilt is concerned with the fact of committing the offence. The crime of a person is estimated by all the circumstances of his conduct which present themselves to observation. His guilt requires to be proved by evidence. The higher the rank of the person, the greater the crime, and the greater the guilt when proven.

In secular terms, a person may commit a crime without being found guilty because of the lack of evidence. With God there is no lack of evidence, and we have been caught redhanded.

A person may be guilty of either the greatest or the smallest of offences. A person may be guilty without committing a crime, such as being guilty of a breach of politeness. Crime is concerned with the thing done, whilst guilt is applied to the person doing.

Illustrations from the Scriptures

Genesis 3 recounts the fall and the guilt of Adam and the woman. That guilt was shown in that fact that they hid themselves, that they were afraid, and that they covered their nakedness. Before the fall they were not conscious of nakedness. Thus today all people dress to cover their nakedness—and that is an admission of their guilt.

Romans chapters 1, 2 and 3 bring before the high court of God the evidence of the witnesses for the prosecution:

The charge Romans 1:18.

The witnesses for the prosecution

The creation 1:19 and 20
Man's choice 1:21 to 27
Man's conduct 1:28 to 32
Man's criticism 2:1 to 11
Man's conscience 2:12 to 16
God's commandments 2:17 to 29.

All objections are overuled in court 3:1 to 9.
No witnesses for the defence.
Summing up by the counsel for the prosecution 3:10 to 18.
The verdict 3:19 and 20 'and all the world may become guilty before God'.

Heart

First mention
Genesis 6:5 'And God saw that the wickedness of man was great in the earth, and that every imagination of the thoughts of his **heart** was only evil continually'.

The reference to thoughts gives the clue to the meaning of the word 'heart'. It refers to the mind, and the very being of man. For instance we talk about heartbreak when we really mean mental anguish.

The word is closely linked with what man really is, i.e. evil and wicked. And it is with this in mind that we preach the gospel.

Synonyms
The soul embraces the subtlest or most ethereal of sensible objects, namely, breath or spirit, and denotes properly the quickening or vital principle.

The mind is that sort of power which is closely allied to, and in a great measure dependent upon, corporeal organization.

The heart represents both man's mental and moral activity; both rational and emotional elements, the hidden springs of the personal life. In the Old Testament it denotes emotions, reason and the will. In the New Testament it denotes the seat of the physical life, moral and spiritual life. It represents the true man, not the outward man.

Illustrations from the Scriptures
Romans 10 deals much with the heart. Verse 1 uses the expression 'my heart's desire' which expresses the emotions. Verse 6 expresses the thoughts in the mind, whilst verse 8 suggests the moral. Verse 9 suggests the whole being, because faith is not just some moral recognition.

Heaven

First mention
Genesis 1:1 'In the beginning God created the **heaven** and the earth'.
Heaven, here, is distinct from earth, a principle that runs through the Scriptures.
It is created by God, and therefore He has complete control over it.

Synonyms
Celestial, from a latin word, denotes the heaven of the heathens. The word heaven has acquired a superior meaning in the habitation of God Himself. Celestial is commonly used in a natural sense, whilst heaven is used in a spiritual sense. Hence we speak of celestial bodies (the stars), whilst we speak of the heavenlies, heavenly joy or bliss, and heavenly spirits.

The Greek words used admit of three heavens:
1. The lower atmosphere of less purer air from the ground to the tops of the mountains.
2. The upper atmosphere of purer air, and the abode of the stars.
3. Heaven itself the habitation of God, and the believer's ultimate goal.

Illustrations from the Scriptures

Luke 16 draws the curtain to one side, and we have a glimpse of Heaven, described as Abraham's bosom. It is a place of comfort and uninterrupted bliss because Lazarus could not leave to attend to the rich man's need in Hell.

Hebrews 9:24 tells us that Heaven answers to the holy place in the tabernacle, which was a figure of the true. He, our great high priest, is in heaven, now to appear in the presence of God on our behalf.

Hell

First mention

Deuteronomy 32:22 'For a fire is kindled in mine anger, and shall burn unto the lowest **hell**, and shall consume the earth with her increase, and set on fire the foundations of the mountains'.

Hell is closely linked with the anger of God, provoked by a forward generation, with no faith, who had moved God to jealousy. It is also linked with fire and a place situated in a low place.

Synonyms

Gulf derives from a word that means hollow, whilst abyss derives from a word that means bottomless. One is overwhelmed in a gulf; it carries with it the idea of profundity, into which one sinks never to rise. One is lost in an abyss; it carries with it the idea of immense profundity, into which he who is cast never reaches a bottom, nor is able to return to the top.

Hell is represented as a fiery gulf (Luke 16) into which the lost are plunged, and remain perpetually overwhelmed.

Hades was the name of the Greek god of the underworld (Latin *Pluto*) and represents, now, the region of the departed spirits of the lost. In time, it is that period between death and the eternal doom of Hell. It never denotes the grave, nor Hell, the permanent region of the lost.

Illustrations from the Scriptures

Nehemiah 3 mentions the dung gate which led to the valley of Hinnom. It was through this gate that the domestic refuse of Jerusalem was taken to be dumped into the valley of Hinnom. It is a known fact that any rubbish dump will experience, in time, spontaneous combustion because of the formation of acetate within the rubbish pile. Thus a rubbish dump is perpetually burning in its depths. The Hebrew for the valley of Hinnom is GE-HINNOM which is transliterated into Greek in the form GEHENNA, and which, in turn is translated in the A.V. by Hell. Thus we have a graphic picture of Hell. It is significant that in Scriptures Heaven cannot be described, but Hell can; as if to give us all a solemn warning of the dangers of Hell.

We cannot but refer to Luke 16 again and see the torment of the rich man, who was dead, yet alive, with all his faculties. He was able to see, recognise, speak and feel. We need to preach to the people what Hell is like. We must warn them of the danger that lies ahead.

Holy

First mention
Exodus 3:5 'And he said, Draw not nigh hither: put off thy shoes from off thy feet, for the place whereon thou standest is **holy** ground'.

The word holy here refers to a place not a person; but, nevertheless, the place is holy becaue of the presence of a holy God. The awesomeness of holiness is to be respectful in the highest degree; to hide the face: and to express fear.

Synonyms
Holiness is unhallowed by a mixture of inferior objects; and is elevated in the greatest possible degree, so as to suit the nature of the infinitely perfect, and exalted being of God. Among the Jews, the holy of holies was that place which was intended to approach the nearest to the heavenly abode (Hebrews 9:24) and consequently was preserved as much as possible from all contamination with that which was earthly.

Sacred is less than holy; the sacred derives its sanction from human institutions, and is connected rather with our moral than our spiritual duties.

That which is sacred may be simply the human purified

from what is gross and corrupt; that which is holy must be regarded with awe, and treated with every possible mark of reverence. A man's word may be sacred, but not holy.

Some writings may be referred to as sacred, but the Scriptures are holy, because they are the Word of God.

Divine expresses that which is not human.

Sacred expresses that which is not common.

Holy expresses that which is not of sin.

Illustrations from the Scriptures

Both the word 'holy' and the word 'sanctification' have the same root which means to separate. Ephesians 5:27 employs the word 'holy' in the sense that the church is to be presentable to God, devoid of spot, wrinkle, and blemish.

2 Peter 1:21 teaches that a holy man is such as is moved by the Holy Spirit, and not governed by the will of man. It stands in contrast to the first verse of chapter 2 which exposes false prophets and false teachers.

Hope

First mention

Ruth 1:12 'Turn again, my daughters, go your way; for I am too old to have an husband. If I should say, I have **hope**, if I should have an husband also to night, and should bear sons'.

Hope is related not to the expectancy of human and natural things, but to things outside the realm of the natural. It is linked with those things that are impossible to man.

Synonyms
Hope is welcome; expectation is either welcome or unwelcome: we hope only for that which is good; we expect the bad as well as the good. In bad weather we hope it will soon be better; but in a bad season we expect a bad harvest, and in a good season a good harvest. The modern usage of the word 'hope' is completely corrupted. Today it seems to express doubt as in 'I hope that it will not rain'. Hope in the Word of God is a sure certainty that it will come to pass—it is relying upon God's Word. It is confidence in His Word. Our salvation depends upon the promises of God (see Galatians 3).

The young man hopes to live many years; the old man expects to die in a few years.

We expect our friends to assist us in a time of need. It is a reasonable expectation founded upon their tried regard for us and promises of assistance.

If we trust that an eminent physician will cure us, it is founded upon our knowledge of his skill, and of the nature of our case.

Trust and confidence agree with hope in regard to the objects anticipated. Trust springs from a view of the circumstances connected with an event; confidence arises more from the temper of the mind than from the nature of the object.

Illustrations from the Scriptures
Romans 4:18 and on looks at Abraham, who against all probability, believed and hoped in the promise. Notice

how faith and hope are linked in Hebrews 11:1. Faith makes the things that God has promised in the future, a reality.

Romans 8:24 states that we are saved by hope, i.e. we have confidence in that which God has promised. Anything that is seen does not require faith or hope because it has come to fruition by the very fact that it can be seen. Thus we hope for the things that as yet are unseen.

Humility

First mention

Exodus 10:3 'And Moses and Aaron came in unto Pharaoh, and said unto him, Thus saith the LORD God of the Hebrews, How long wilt thou refuse to **humble** thyself before me? let my people go, that they may serve me'.

Humility is set in contrast to stubborness and refusal. It is that which reacts against the flesh, and that against which the flesh reacts. It is not the natural state of man, and is opposed by man's status, pride, and achievement. But humility is essential to serving God and doing His will.

Synonyms

A person is said to be humble on account of the state of his mind; he is said to be lowly either on account of his mind or his outward circumstances.

Humility should form part of the character, as it is opposed to arrogance and assumption; lowliness should form a part of our temper, as it is opposed to an aspiring and lofty mind. The humble and the lowly are always taken in a good sense. A lowly man, whether as it respects his mind or his condition, is so without any moral debasement. But a man who is low in his condition is likewise conceived to be low in his habits and his sentiments. A humble station is associated with the highest moral worth; whilst a low office, a low situation, a low birth seem to exclude the idea of worth.

The humble is so with regard to ourselves or others: modesty is that which respects ourselves only; submissiveness that which respects others. A man is humble from a sense of his comparative inferiority to others in point of station and outward circumstances; or he is humble from a sense of his imperfections, and a consciousness of not being what he ought to be. He is modest in as much as he sets but little value on his qualifications, acquirements, endowments.

Humility marks a temper of the mind; submissiveness a mode of action. Humility is therefore often the cause of submissiveness. A man is humble in his closet when he takes a review of his sinfulness: he is submissive to a master whom he desires to please.

We can talk about a humble air and a submissive air. The former to denote a man's sense of his own comparative littleness, the latter to indicate his readiness to be resigned to the will of another.

Humility is commonly used of persons: whilst humiliation of things. No man humbles himself by the acknowledgement of a fault: but it is a great humiliation for a person to be dependent on another for a living when he has it in his power to obtain it for himself.

To humble is to bring down to the ground: to degrade is to let down lower.

A lesson in the school of adversity is humbling.

A lesson in the school of warfare is humiliating, when terms of peace are sought.

Low vices are peculiarly degrading to a man of rank.

Illustrations from the Scriptures

Philippians 2 strikes the chord for us. Humility is seen as a particular state of the mind. Verse 3 employs the expression 'lowliness of mind' in esteeming others better than oneself. It is an unconscious self forgetfulness. It is something of which we cannot be aware. There can be no pride of humility, because it is a contradiction of terms. It was not a question of Christ humbling Himself to become a man, for man can be proud. But as a man He humbled himself. Let THIS mind be in you, which was also in Christ Jesus.

Iniquity

First mention

Genesis 15:16 'But in the fourth generation they shall come hither again: for the **iniquity** of the Amorites is not yet full'.

In the light of the fact that the iniquity of the Amorites was not yet full implies an ongoing thing—a state, a condition.

Synonyms

Wickedness is the generic term, and iniquity signifies

that species of wickedness that violates the law. It is lawlessness and the want of equity and fairness. Nefarious is that species of wickedness which consists in violating the most sacred obligations.

It is wicked to deprive another of his property unlawfully, under any circumstances; but it is iniquitous if it be done by fraud and circumvention; and nefarious if it involves any breach of trust.

Illustrations from the Scriptures

Isaiah 53 affords some clues about the meaning of the word. It is set in contrast with the Righteous Servant justifying many in verse 11. Therefore it is unrighteousness.

The chapter mentions frequently the word transgression and puts it by the side of iniquity in verse 5. Iniquity, as we have already said, is lawlessness. Transgression is the act of going beyond the law. Trespass is the act of passing beyond. The latter terms are very similar. (See further on in the book under Transgression and Trespass).

Inspiration

First mention

Job 32:8 'But there is a spirit in man: and the **inspiration** of the Almighty giveth them understanding'.

It is set by the side of the spirit of man, and it is an attribute of God. It gives man understanding, and when applied to the Scriptures we must realise that the Word of God is about God to man, and is written by God as God.

Synonyms

Inspiration signifies to breathe life or spirit into. Whilst the word is used in secular circles with a meaning more akin to animate and enliven, in Scripture the word clearly means God-breathed.

Illustrations from the Scriptures

2 Timothy 3:16 shows that the inspiration of Scripture is:

1. Inclusive   — **All** Scripture
2. Exclusive   — All **Scripture**
3. Conclusive — profitable for doctrine, for reproof, for correction, for instruction in righteousness.

2 Peter 1:20 and 21 tells us what inspiration is not. There is no room for private interpretation. But holy men, holy, please note, were moved, borne along as a sailing ship in the wind, by the Holy Spirit.

Jealousy

First mention

Exodus 20:5 'Thou shalt not bow down thyself to them, nor serve them: for I the LORD thy God am a **jealous** God, visiting the iniquity of the fathers upon the children unto the third and fourth generation of them that hate me.'

The word jealous is first attributed to God, not man, and He claims allegiance and loyalty from His people to the exclusion of all rival deities.

JEALOUSY

Synonyms

Jealousy impies being filled with a burning desire, the word 'zealous' being a related word. Envy signifies looking at something in a contrary direction.

We are jealous of that which is our own: we are envious of that which is another's.

Jealousy fears to lose what it has: envy is pained at seeing another have.

Princes are jealous of their authority; subjects are jealous of their rights: courtiers are envious of those in favour; women can be envious of superior beauty.

The jealous man has an object of desire, something to get and something to retain.

The envious man sickens at the sight of enjoyment; he is easy only in the misery of others; all endeavours, therefore, to satisfy an envious man are fruitless.

Jealousy is a noble passion (God is a jealous God: He, alone, had the right to claim the people He had redeemed). Envy is always a base passion, having the worst passions in its train.

Illustrations from the Scriptures

2 Corinthians 11:2 talks of godly jealousy, a jealousy on a higher plain than human jealousy. It is not that Paul had the right to possess them, but they belonged to Christ, in the manner of a chaste virgin espoused to but one husband.

Joy

First mention
Deuteronomy 28:47 'Because thou servedst not the LORD thy God with **joyfulness**, and with gladness of heart, for the abundance of all things.'

The reason for the curses outlined in this chapter is because of the disobedience of the children of God. Therefore joy is linked with obedience to the will of God, and the great privelege of serving Him. Experience has proved that the path of true and lasting joy is obedience to His will, and serving Him with gladness of heart.

Synonyms
Both joy and gladness lie internally, whilst mirth and happiness are the more immediate result of external circumstances. That which creates joy and gladness is of a permanent nature; that which creates mirth and happiness is temporary.

Joy is the most vivid sensation in the soul: joy is awakened in the mind by the most important events in life.

Gladness is the same in quality as joy, but inferior only in degree. The return of the prodigal son awakened joy in the heart of the father: but a man feels gladness at being relieved from some distress, or trouble.

Joy is a tranquil feeling which is employed in secret, and seeks no outward expression: mirth displays itself in laughter, singing, and noise.

Illustrations from the Scriptures
The joy mentioned in Romans 5:11 is closely linked in

the context of this chapter, with the facts of our salvation. The outline on the chapter looks like this:
1. **Fruits of Salvation** verses 1 to 5
2. **Foundation of Salvation** verses 6 to 11
3. **Facts of Salvation** verses 12 to 21.

Joy depends upon facts, not feelings. Mirth and happiness depend upon feelings, not facts. The effects that mirth and happiness produce can be simulated by the inhaling of laughing gas. Even when good feelings have gone, the facts are still there, and I have joy.

Judgment

First mention
Genesis 15:14 'And also that nation, whom they shall serve, will I **judge**: and afterward shall they come out with great substance.'

Judgment here is in relation to the treatment of God's people, and is the result of the action of the taskmasters of Egypt. The judgment is based on knowledge of the circumstances and is able to distinguish right from wrong.

Synonyms
The terms judgment, discretion, and prudence are all employed to express the various modes of practical wisdom which serve to regulate the conduct of men in ordinary life.

Judgment is that faculty which enables a person to distinguish right and wrong. Judgment is conclusive; it decides by positive inference: it enables a person to discover the truth. Discretion is intuitive (compare discernment); it discerns or perceives what is in all probability right. Judgment acts by fixed rule; it admits of no question or variation: discretion acts according to circumstances, and its own rule. Judgment requires knowledge and actual experience: discretion requires reflection and consideration.

Discretion looks to the present: prudence calculates on the future. We must have prudence when we have discretion, but we may have prudence where there is no occasion for discretion. For want of discretion the general of an army may lose his authority: for want of prudence the businessman may involve himself in ruin.

Illustrations from the Scriptures

In John 5:22 the only Being in the universe of God who has a right to judge the sinner is exalted to be a Saviour now. The day of grace must end before the day of judgment can begin. 'The acceptable year of the Lord must run its course before the advent of 'the day of vengeance'. Compare Isaiah 61 verses 1 and 2 with Luke 4:16 and 20. The Lord closed the book in mid sentence, for there is no comma in the Hebrew language. The day of vengeance waits on the day of grace.

Romans 2:6 to 11 show that God's judgments are according to pure equity.

The distinction between judgment (sentence pronounced) and punishment (sentence executed) has already been made under the heading of condemnation, and in the context of John 3:18. In 2 Corinthians 5:18 and on, we learn that reconciliation is for all. Then how is judgment possible? Judgment is based upon this very truth. Sin is now no longer against the law merely, it is against grace. Light has come into the world and man has ignored the argument in John 3.

Justification

First mention

Exodus 23:7 'Keep thee far from a false matter; and the innocent and righteous slay thou not; for I will not **justify** the wicked.'

Thus speaks the law. The context reveals a series of acts that the child of God was forbidden to do. No matter how plausible the excuse, there was to be no justification for disobeying the commandments of God. Remember that God is a righteous God and in declaring a person not guilty, declares that person as being righteous. He must be able to maintain His righteous integrity. The first suggestion of that great theme, justification by faith, is seen in Genesis 15:6, which Paul mentions in Romans 4, showing that the gospel is as old as Abraham.

Synonyms

To justify is to declare as not guilty; to declare as righteous. This does not mean that God winks at sin and turns the other way. Romans 3:26 makes this point clearly when it states: 'that He might be just, and the justifier of him that believeth in Jesus'. Through the death of Christ on the cross and His resurrection from the dead, God can make the sinner clean, and still maintain His righteous integrity.

Justification is not a reprieve, it is more than pardon: I am declared not guilty. Romans 8:33 'Who shall lay any thing to the charge of God's elect? It is God that justifieth'. A judge who sets a man free, although he has been proved guilty, becomes a partaker of the crime. This is not the case with God. The prisoner has been set free, but the price has been paid, the debt settled, for Christ has died, yea has risen again from the dead. Romans 4:25 'Who was delivered for our offences and was raised again for our justification'. Thus justification is not condoning sin.

Defend signifies to keep or ward off. Excuse signifies to get out of any cause or affair. Justify signifies to do justice and to put it right.

Illustrations from the Scriptures

We can do no better than to draw from Romans 3, 4 and 5. We **first** learn that justification is by grace. This means that it is free, and that it comes to the sinner undeserved. There is no room for boasting. It is by grace, and God is not robbed of His glory thereby.

Secondly we are justified by faith, that means it is not by the law, or by works. Not that faith is any kind of merit for 'it is of faith, that it might be by grace' Romans 4:16. The parable of the Pharisee and the Publican teaches that faith is the means by which we receive, not give; hence the publican goes down to his house justified.

Thirdly justification is by blood (Romans 5:9) and thus guilt that sin produces is taken away. Let Satan jibe me as much as he cares—my guilt is gone, and the shed blood of Christ is the reason.

Fourthly justification is by works. This seems to

KINGDOM 67

negate all that has been laid down by Paul—but not according to James. It is the complement of justification by faith. It is justification by faith in the sight of God; justification by works in the sight of man. Thus justification by works, according to James' owns grace and does homage to the blood.

Kingdom

First mention
Kingdom (in the context of our subject) Exodus 19:6 'And ye shall be unto me a **kingdom** of priests, and an holy nation. These are the words which thou shalt speak unto the children of Israel.'

The word is used with regard to obeying God's voice, letting God rule over His people, keeping His covenants. It is employed with particular reference to His own people, and His sovereignty over the earth.

Kingdom of Heaven Matthew 3:2 'And saying, Repent ye: for the **kingdom of heaven** is at hand.' The Lord's ministry began by an announcement that the promised rule was about to come. This verse was not the statement of a present truth or fact, but a prophetic declaration. This was the purpose of the first gospel. It is the gospel of the Kingdom of heaven; for the expression is peculiar to Matthew, who uses it 33 times, meaning always and only the promised Messianic earthly kingdom.

Kingdom of God Matthew 6:33 'But seek ye first the **kingdom of God**, and his righteousness; and all these things shall be added unto you.'

Surprisingly the first mention of the expression 'kingdom of God' occurs in a gospel that is devoted to the gospel of the kingdom of heaven. The context will show that here the expression 'kingdom of God' must be used and not the expression 'kingdom of heaven'.

Synonyms
The only thing we can do here is to differentiate between the two expressions: 'kingdom of heaven' and 'kingdom of God'.

Kingdom of heaven
Means the promised Messianic earthly kingdom, as already stated.

Kingdom of God
In this expression the word 'kingdom' has no longer a fixed meaning. In some passages it means the rule of God; in others, the whole sphere in which that rule is exercised; and in others again it has an ethical or spiritual meaning, as representing the state of blessedness pertaining to the Divine Rule.

Illustrations from the Scriptures
Kingdom of Heaven
As we have said this expression is peculiar to Matthew's gospel, occuring no less than 33 times, and occurs nowhere else in the New Testament. The word kingdom occurs 54 times in the book of Daniel, and it is in this book that we have the key to the meaning of the expression. That the heavens rule was announced to Nebuchadnezzar as a present fact and truth (Daniel 4:26). But chapter 2 and 7 foretold a future kingdom upon this earth, when God would take back the sceptre of earthly sovereignty.

Kingdom of God

This expression occurs 5 times in Matthew; 15 times in Mark; 33 times in Luke; twice in John; 7 times in Acts, and occasionally in the epistles.

John 3:3 and 5 affords a notable instance of the meaning; an ethical or spiritual meaning, as representing the state of blessedness. To substitute the phrase 'kingdom of heaven' would be wrong and would not make any sense.

Knowledge

First mention

Genesis 2:9 'And out of the ground made the LORD God to grow every tree that is pleasant to the sight, and good for food; the tree of life also in the midst of the garden, and the tree of **knowledge** of good and evil.'

The basis of all knowledge is the ability to differentiate between good and evil, right and wrong, truth and error.

Synonyms

Knowledge is a general term. Learning is that species of knowledge which one derives from schools, or through the medium of personal instruction.

We know a man to be good or bad, virtuous or vicious, by being a witness to his actions: we become acquainted with him by frequently being in his company.

Knowledge is a familiarity gained by experience, seeking to know is the sense of enquiry, and investigation.

Illustrations from the Scriptures

Philippians 3:8 expresses Paul's great ambition for the excellency of the knowledge of Christ Jesus his Lord. The ensuing verses explain what that implies. To be found in Him is the knowledge of Him, to be seen, and to be discovered in Him. To know Him means to know the power of His resurrection in my life. To know Him means the fellowship of His sufferings, bearing in my body the marks of the Lord Jesus, having God's signature on my life. To know Him means being made conformable unto His death, the reproduction of the cross of Christ in my life.

Law

First mention

Genesis 26:5 'Because that Abraham obeyed my voice, and kept my charge, my commandments, my statutes, and my **laws**.'

The word is linked with obeying God's voice, with keeping a charge like a deposit; with commandments, and with statutes.

Synonyms

The precept derives its authority from the individual delivering it; in this manner the precepts of the Lord Jesus Christ have a weight which gives them a decided superiority over everything else. The rule acquires a worth from its fitness for guiding us in our life. The law derives its weight from the sanction of power. Maxims are often precepts in as much as they are communicated to us by our parents. A maxim is a moral truth that carries its own weight with itself. Precept, rule, and law signify the thing specifically chosen or marked out, all borrowing their weight from some external circumstance.

Illustrations from the Scriptures

Galatians chapters 3 and 4 are devoted to the function of the law, and the key verse is 3:19: 'Wherefore serveth the law?' The law like the pedagogue brought us to Christ that we might be justified by faith. By faith, please note, NOT by the law. For when faith came we were no longer under such a schoolmaster; and our relationship to God stands by faith in Christ Jesus.

The outline of the two chapters is given below, and will repay careful study:

a. **The Law and Conversion** 3:1 to 9
b. **The Law and the Curse** 3:10 to 14
c. **The Law and the Covenant** 3:15 to 18
d. **The Law and Sin** 3:19 to 23
e. **The Law and Christ** 3:24 to 29
f. **The Law and Children** 4:1 to 7
g. **The Law and the Calendar** 4:8 to 11
h. **The Law and its Cohorts** 4:12 to 31.

Romans, closely allied to Galatians in thought, expresses death to sin in chapter 6, death to the law in chapter 7, and death to the flesh in chapter 8.

Romans 7:7 states that it was through the law that there was a knowledge of sin. But the law is holy in itself (verse 12) and it dragged sin into recognition, making sin exceedingly sinful (verse 13). Thus the advent of the law made the sinner a transgressor.

Liberty

First mention

Leviticus 25:10 'And ye shall hallow the fiftieth year, and proclaim **liberty** throughout all the land unto all the inhabitants thereof: it shall be a jubilee unto you; and ye shall return every man unto his family.'

Liberty, here, is freedom with responsibility, because they were to make the returns as specified in the verse. Liberty is NOT a licence for a believer to do as he pleases.

Synonyms

Freedom is personal and private; liberty is public. Freedom of a city is the privilege granted by the city to the individual: the liberties of the city are immunities enjoyed by the city. By the same rule of distinction we speak of the freedom of the will, the freedom of conversation, or freedom of debate; but the liberty of conscience, the liberty of the press, the liberty of the subject.

Freedom serves moreover to qualify the action: liberty is applied only to the agent. Hence we say, to speak or think with freedom: but to have liberty of speaking, thinking, or acting.

Illustrations from the Scriptures

Galatians chapter 5 affords some important points on the subject of liberty. Verse 13 states that such liberty is not to be used as an occasion to the flesh. In other words, liberty does not become a base of operations for the display of the flesh. It must be freedom with responsibility. I must love my neighbour: I must consider others. Verse 15 means that contest will not end in victory to either party. It will lead to the common extinction of both.

Life eternal

First mention (the word 'life' alone)
Genesis 1:20 'And God said, Let the waters bring forth abundantly the moving creature that hath **life**, and fowl that may fly above the earth in the open firmament of heaven.'

Although the word 'life' here is concerned with the creatures, the principle is still the same: all life comes from God. He is the sole author of life, and although man is striving to achieve this process, he will never succeed.

Synonyms

Existence is the property of all things in the universe: life is the inherent power of God bestowed by Him upon His creatures.

Plants have life because they grow.

Animals have life because they grow and think.

Man has life because he grows, thinks and is conscious of a God—he is a moral being.

Exist, therefore is the general term, whilst live is the specific term. Whatever lives, exists according to a certain mode: but many things exist without living.

When we wish to speak of things in their most abstract relation, we say they exist: when we wish to characterize the form of existence, we say they live. Life is employed to denote an active principle.

Illustrations from the Scriptures

In contrast to eternal death as already outlined in Luke chapter 15 and 16 under the heading of 'death', we see that eternal life is its antithesis i.e. **no** separation and alienation from God. Not for one second of time was Lazarus allowed to leave his eternal bliss to cater for the needs of the rich man in Hell.

That well known verse in John 3:16 states that we **have** (as a present possession) everlasting life, through faith in Christ. It is not for the future, it is for the present, and there is no separation from God.

Romans 8:35 puts it right for us: 'Who shall separate us from the love of Christ?' The answer in the context is that nothing can!

Light

First mention

Genesis 1:3 'And God said, Let there be **light**: and there was **light**.'

This was God's first commandment. God alone can give true light. It is separate and distinct from darkness. The two cannot exist together.

Synonyms

Illumination suggests artificial light. The word 'light' in the context of our subject is not only natural light, but spiritual light.

LIGHT

Artificial, man-made light, can deceive the eye with respect to form and colour. Thus light by the standard of man can deceive: but no country is considered enlightened unless it has received the light of the Gospel of Christ.

Illustrations from the Scriptures

It is used:

a. as the Glory of God's dwelling place—1 Timothy 6:16
b. as the very nature of God—1 John 1:5
c. as the impartiality of God—James 1:17
d. of Christ in relation to sinful man—John 8:12
e. with respect to the power of the Scriptures—Psalm 119:115
f. with respect to the guidance of God—Psalm 112:4
g. with respect to salvation—1 Peter 2:9
h. with respect to witnessing for God—Matthew 5:14 and 16.

From John chapter 8 we learn more about the Light of the World, Christ.

a. it exposes and reveals—verse 9
b. it reflects—verse 11 'go and sin no more'
c. it is pure—verse 16 'my judgement is true'
d. it warns—verse 24 'ye shall die in your sins'
e. it is elevated that all may enjoy it—verse 28 'when ye have lifted up the Son of Man'.
f. it guides—verse 32 'ye shall know the truth', and in chapter 9.
g. light can be shut out—verse 40 and 41 'are we blind also?', 'your sin remaineth'.

Love

First mention

Genesis 22:2 'And he said, Take now thy son, thine only son Isaac, whom thou **lovest**, and get thee into the land of Moriah; and offer him there for a burnt offering upon one of the mountains which I will tell thee of.'

Love, here, is seen as the deep relationship between a father and his only son. His only son in the sense that Isaac was **the** son of promise, and not the son of the flesh. It is a love that is very closely linked with obedience: 'Take now thy son'; 'If ye love me, keep my commandments' John 14:15.

Synonyms (as employed of our feelings to each other and to God)

A person is affectionate who has the object of his regard strongly in his mind, who participates in his pleasures and pains, and is pleased with society. A person is kind who expresses a tender sentiment, or does any service in a pleasant manner. A person is fond, who caresses an object, or makes it a source of pleasure to himself.

Love and affection express two sentiments of the heart which do honour to human nature: they are the bonds by which mankind are knit together. We cannot love without affection, but we may have affection without love.

Love is the natural sentiment between near relations: affection subsists between those who are less intimately connected, being the consequence of friendship.

Love is powerful in its effects, awakening great things in the human frame. Affection is a chastened feeling under the control of the understanding.

LOVE

Love subsists between members of the same family; it springs out of their natural relationship, and is kept alive by their close and constant interchange of kindnesses.

Friendship excludes the idea of any tender and natural relationship; it is governed by time, circumstances, and the character of person involved as the object of our friendship.

Love is peculiar to no station; it is to be found equally among the high and the low, the learned and the unlearned.

Love is exclusive in its nature; it insists upon a devotion to a single object; it is jealous of any intrusion from others (look up the word 'jealousy' in this book).

Illustrations from the Scriptures

The remarks under the heading of synonyms have dealt with love on a lower level. When talking about the love of God, we are on an infinitely higher level, where the word takes on a new meaning, a meaning that the world cannot understand or recognise.

John 3:16 shows that the true meaning of love is the giving of everything. For God, it was the giving of His only begotten Son.

1 John 3:1 asks the question: 'Behold, what manner of love?' This literally means what is this that comes from another country? God's love is foreign to the way of this world. It is a love that sacrifices everything, holding nothing back. As God towards us; as the Son towards His bride: as the believer to another believer. Our love for each other is inspired by His love for us.

Mediator

First mention

Galatians 3:19 'Wherefore then serveth the law? It was added because of transgression, till the seed should come to whom the promise was made; and it was ordained by angels in the hand of a **mediator**.'

Also verse 20. 'Now a **mediator** is not a **mediator** of one, but God is one.'

Thus we learn that a mediator functions between two parties in order to produce the desired effect.

The angels shared in the giving of the law (q.v. Deuteronomy 33:2 'saints' mean angels), and the mediator referred to in verse 19 is Moses (q.v. Hebrews 8:6 and the mediator of a better covenant, which is Christ in contrast to Moses).

Looking at verse 20, a mediator implies a contract to two parties, where a contract implies conditions. If the conditions are not observed, then all fails. The law has not been kept, and the blessings have been forfeited. But the promise depends on God ONLY. Hence the phrase, 'God is one.'

Synonyms

Intercede signifies literally going between.
Interpose signifies placing one's self between.
Mediate signifies coming in the middle.
Interfere signifies setting one's self between.
Intermeddle signifies mixing among.

One intercedes between parties that are unequal; one interposes between parties that are equal. One intercedes in favour of a party which is threatened with punishments; one interposes between parties that threaten each other with evil.

One intercedes by means of persuasion: one interposes by an exercise of authority.

One mediates for the attainment of good. A mediator guarantees; he takes upon himself responsibility.

Christ is our Intercessor by virtue of His resurrection from the dead.

Christ is our Mediator by virtue of His death upon the cross.

Interfere and intermeddle are said of what concerns only one individual.

Intercede, interpose, and mediate are said in cases of two or more parties.

Illustrations from the Scriptures

1 Timothy 2:5 shows the mediator must possess the nature and the attribute of both sides, i.e. the Man, Christ Jesus. God and Man—beyond human reasoning, but the only hope for mankind. And there is ONE mediator—any other will not do, for it robs God of His glory.

Memorial

First mention

Exodus 3:15 'And God said moreover unto Moses, Thus shalt thou say unto the children of Israel, The LORD God of your fathers, the God of Abraham, the God of Isaac, and the God of Jacob hath sent me unto you: this is my name for ever, and this is my **memorial** unto all generations.'

The word is linked with God's covenant name, Jehovah, and the idea in the word is to look both into the past and into the future. Into the past, for God is the God of Abraham, Isaac, and Jacob: into the future, 'unto all generations.'

The word also has another dimension in as much as it suggests a part of the whole, and that part being consistent with the whole. (See under, in illustrations from the Scriptures). Thus in our text, the name of God, being the part, is consistent with the whole, being God Himself. He is as good as His name. He is all that all His names imply. Here, His name implies that He is the God of the living, not the dead; He is the God that makes the promises and keeps them.

Synonyms

A monument signifies that which puts us in mind of something.
A memorial signifies the thing that helps the memory.
A monument is used to preserve a public object of notice from being forgotten.
A memorial serves to keep an individual in mind.

Memorials are more of a private nature than monuments, and they respect something or somebody external to ourselves. The memorial revives in our minds what we owe to another: and carries us back to another.

Illustrations from the Scriptures

Leviticus 2:2, in the context of the meal offering, mentions the word 'memorial' in the sense of the part of the whole, and that part being consistent with the whole. This idea is to be found in Acts 10:4 in the narrative which concerns Cornelius. His prayers and alms were a memorial in the sense that they were consistent with the rest of his life.

Mercy

First mention
Genesis 19:16 'And while he lingered, the men laid hold upon his hand, and upon the hand of his wife, and upon the hand of his two daughters; the LORD being **merciful** unto him: and they brought him forth, and set him without the city.'

The word is used in connection with Lot escaping from Sodom and represents God holding back from man that which he deserves. Compare this definition with that of grace: grace is God giving to us that which we do not deserve.

Synonyms
Pity is often a sentiment unaccompanied with action: mercy is accompanied with action. We take pity upon a person, but we show mercy to a person. Pity is bestowed by men in their domestic and private capacity: mercy is shown in the exercise of power.

God takes pity on us as entire dependants upon Him: He extends His mercy towards us as offenders against Him. He shows His pity by relieving our wants: He shows His mercy by forgiving our sins.

Clemency lies in the disposition: mercy lies in the act. A monarch may display his clemency by showing mercy.

Illustrations from the Scriptures
Mercy is at the discretion of God. Romans 9:15 states:

'I will have mercy on whom I will have mercy': we are thrown back upon the sovereignty of God here. Our salvation depends upon the mercy of God. Titus 3:5 states: 'Not by works of righteousness which we have done, but according to His mercy He saved us...'

In the parable of the Pharisee and the Publican in Luke 18, it was mercy that the man needed because he was a sinner. This plea harks back to the mercy seat in the holy place, in the tabernacle. There was a necessity for the shedding of blood; and shed blood means death applied, and that death, the death of the Lord Jesus Christ upon the cross. This is the basis: this is the only way.

Miracle

First mention
Exodus 7:9 'When Pharaoh shall speak unto you, saying, Shew a **miracle** for you: then thou shalt say unto Aaron, Take thy Rod, and cast it before Pharaoh, and it shall become a serpent'.

This verse shows that the miracle that would be performed, would be performed by the express permission of God. It was NOT for some cheap entertainment, but it was, in itself, a message from God to the king.

Synonyms
Wonders are natural, in the sense that creation is full of such wonders. But, having said that, in Scripture the word 'wonder' is used of a miracle in the sense that it is

MIRACLE

of supernatural origin, and it cannot be explained.

Wonders are real, but marvels are often fictitious, whilst prodigies are extravagant and imaginery.

Wonders can be agreeable to the laws of nature, but when the word is used as a miracle, it can be contrary to the laws of nature, e.g. 2 Kings 6 the axe head that floated, the sun standing still in the days of Joshua, and the backwards movement of the shadow in the days of Hezekiah.

The production of a tree from a grain of seed is a wonder; but the production of an animal with two heads is a monstrosity.

The word 'sign' can also be used for a miracle, in the sense that the miracle is performed with a view to giving the people a message.

Illustrations from the Scriptures

John chapter 6 has got to be a classic example, where we read of the feeding of the multitude. The miracle was a sign, it was a message for the people. Verse 27 reads: 'Labour not for the meat which perisheth, but for that meat which endureth unto everlasting life, which the Son of Man shall give unto you'. In other words, the miracle was a wonderful object lesson to the people, to encourage them to pursue the spiritual food, and to feed on Christ. Mark chapter 8 records the miracle of a man who was blind, but there was no immediate cure, for, at first, the man saw men as trees walking. The sceptic will leap on this and complain that something had gone wrong. The sceptic cannot see that the miracle was a sign, i.e. it was a message to His disciples. The man could not see clearly, and the disciples could not see clearly, spiritually. Peter showed a measure of spiritual discernment, in that he announced that Jesus was the Christ. But in the next breath he refused to accept the cross, and the suffering before the glory. He still could not see clearly.

Mystery

First mention
Matthew 13:11 'He answered and said unto them, Because it is given unto you to know the **mysteries** of the kingdom of heaven, but to them it is not given'.

This statement is a direct answer to the disciples' question in verse 10; 'Why speakest Thou unto them in parables?' One most important definition of the word is seen here, even on the surface, and that is some could know the mysteries of God, and some could not. Those that knew responded to the revelation of God, whilst those that knew not, did not respond to that same revelation.

Synonyms
That which is secret is known to some, and not to others. It is this idea that is behind the scriptural meaning of the word 'mystery', in as much as the believer has been initiated into secrets.

That which is hidden may be known by no one.

A secret concerns only the individual or individuals who hold it; but that which is hidden may concern the whole world.

That which is secret is often not known to be secret: but that which is a mystery is so only in the eyes of others.

MYSTERY

The date of the rapture of the church, and all that it means, is a secret, but not a mystery to the believer.

Mystery is applied to the supernatural, disclosed by divine revelation.

Mystics is applied to the natural (as far as the world is concerned) concealed by an artificial or fantastical veil.

Illustrations from the Scriptures

The word finds its origin in a Greek verb which means 'to shut the mouth', and in Philippians 4:12 it means to be disciplined in a practical lesson. The word has been borrowed from secular Greek use, and elevated to a higher, and spiritual plane. Eleusis, a city 11 miles outside of Athens, was the place that favoured citizens visited to be initiated into mysteries that were most sacred in Greece for over 1,000 years, bringing us to the 4th century A.D. Every year, at the beginning of August, a grand procession would take the sacred way that led to the temple of Ceres, the most splendid of its kind in the world. It was the citizen's duty to withdraw attention from the business and the pleasures of this world. Thus Paul borrows the word, to gain a spiritual point.

The use of the word is most explicit in 1 Corinthians 15:51 'Behold, I **shew** you a mystery'. And again in Romans 11:25 'For I would not, brethren, that ye should be ignorant of this mystery'. And yet again in Colossians 1:26 'Even the mystery which hath been hid from ages and from generations, but now is made manifest to his saints'.

Name

First mention
Genesis 4:26 'and to Seth, to him also there was born a son; and he called his name Enos: then began men to call upon the **name** of the LORD'.

This chapter, like the book, is one of beginnings. It deals with the beginnings of pastoral and agricultural life, of sacrificial offerings, of murder, of music, of metal work, and more to the point here, the beginnings of ordered worship. Man began to call upon the name of the LORD.

Synonyms
Name implies something more specific than reputation. Reputation is acquired only by time, and built only on merit. A name is given, but reputation is not given, but built up in the passing of time. A person may get a name by some specific exploit, but reputation is built up over many years. An inanimate object may be given a name, but reputation is applied only to a person.

A manufacturer has a name for the excellence of a particular article of his own making; a book has a name among those who appreciate literature. But both the manufacturer and the writer have to establish a good reputation.

Illustrations from the Scriptures
In Matthew 1:23 and 25 we see the word 'name' as the proper name of a person. In Luke 1:31, Thou shalt call His name Jesus. This was the name and no other.

Revelation 3:1 suggests that the word is used as of a

reputation 'Thou hast a name that thou livest, and art dead'. What kind of reputation has your assembly?

Matthew 6:9. It is used as representative of a person. The names of God and of His Son tell us more and more about the person of God, and the person of His Son. Even the Holy Spirit of God has many names, that tell us about His person and His work.

Matthew 7:22, and other references suggest that the word is used as the author of a commission.

Matthew 10:41 uses the word as someone being possessed of a certain character. 'He that receiveth a prophet in the name of a prophet shall receive a prophet's reward'.

Obedience

First mention
Genesis 27:8 'Now therefore, my son, **obey** my voice according to that which I command thee'.

We learn from this verse, alone, that obedience involves hearing God's voice in connection with His commands and acting upon it.

Synonyms
One is obedient to a command, but submissive to the will of another. Obedience is always taken in a good sense, and is a course of conduct conformable to the express will of another. Submission is often a personal act, immediately directed to the individual.

We show our obedience to the law by avoiding the

breach of it; we show our obedience to the will of God by making that will the rule of our life.

Obedience and submission impose a restraint on one's own will, in order to bring it into accordance with that of another.

We are obedient from a sense of right; we are submissive from a sense of necessity.

Love to God is followed by obedience to His will; they are coincident virtues that reciprocally act on each other.

Illustrations from the Scriptures

In Matthew 21:28 to 31 we read of the parable of the two sons. The first, when asked to work in his father's vineyard, was quite rude, as well as rebellious, and replied 'I will not'. The second son was most polite and replied, 'I go, sir', but changed his mind. The point is that it was the rebellious son that did the will of his father, because he repented. Apart from heaven being full of sinners (saved by grace), heaven is going to be full of rebellious people (who repented and did the will of God).

King Saul did not completely obey the voice of God. Thus in 1 Samuel 15:22 Samuel reminds Saul: 'Behold, to obey is better than sacrifice, and to hearken than the fat of rams'.

Partial obedience is no obedience at all.

Parable

First mention

Numbers 23:7 'And he took up his **parable**, and said, Balak the king of Moab hath brought me from Aram, out of the mountain of the east, saying, Come, curse me Jacob, and come, defy Israel'.

Notice in verse 5 that the Lord put a word in Balaam's mouth. Balaam's ass spoke contrary to nature, whilst Balaam spoke contrary to his own will. Here the narrative that follows verse 7 is drawn from nature and human circumstances to emphasise a spiritual lesson.

Synonyms

The word 'parable' denotes something thrown or laid beside for the sake of comparison. The hearer must catch the analogy if he is to be instructed by it.

Both parable and allegory imply a veiled mode of speech serving to more or less conceal the main object of the discourse by presenting it under the appearance of something else, which accords with it in most particulars. The parable is mostly employed for moral purposes, whilst the allegory is mostly employed in describing historical events.

The parable substitutes some other subject or agent, who is represented under a character that is suitable to the one referred to.

Figure comes from the Latin word 'to feign' and properly denotes anything painted or feigned by the mind. (The word 'figure' in the Scriptures is better translated by the word 'type').

Metaphor denotes a transfer of one object to another.

Emblem denotes the thing stamped on as a mark.

Symbol denotes the thing cast or conceived in the mind, from its analogy to represent something else.

Type denotes an image of something that is stamped on something else. Hence the offering of Isaac is said to be a type of the offering of Christ.

Illustrations from the Scriptures
The parables of the Lord Jesus Christ abound in the gospel, and each one is a study in itself. Luke 15 rather than being three parables, is to be read as one big parable.

The sheep   Lost from the fold. Knew it was lost, but could find its way home.
The silver   Lost by the fireside. Did not know it was lost.
The son   Lost in a far country. Knew he was lost, and knew the way home.

The last remarks of the prodigal son's father lead the way into chapter 16 and the narrative concerning the rich man and Lazarus. The son dead, yet alive: the rich man was dead, yet alive.

Pardon

First mention
Exodus 23:21 'Beware of him, and obey his voice, provoke him not; for he will not **pardon** your transgressions: for my name is in him'.

This reference speaks about an angel, and teaches that

only God can pardon. The word is employed in connection with transgressions, iniquity, and therefore, sin. God forgives as a Father, but pardons as a judge.

Synonyms

Forgive is compounded from 'for' and 'give', whilst pardon is similarly compounded, but from the French. They both signify not to give the punishment that is due. The main difference in the both words has already been mentioned above, and throws a stress on relationship. Individuals forgive each other personal offences; they pardon offences against law and morals.

The pardon of sin obliterates that which is past, and restores the sinner to the Divine favour; it is promised throughout Scripture to all men on the condition of faith and repentance. Remission of sin alone averts the vengeance of God, which otherwise would fall upon those who are guilty of it.

Illustrations from the Scriptures

This word belongs to the Old Testament. It is constantly used in connection with sin, iniquity, and transgressions, and God is speaking as a judge.

Psalm 25:11 is a typical example of how the word is used. It is employed in connection with the psalmist's iniquity, which even he deems to be great. The plea is to God, for He alone can pardon sin. The plea is also for the sake of the name of God, for such pardon MUST be consistent with the righteous integrity of God.

Peace

First mention

Genesis 15:15 'And thou shalt go to thy fathers in **peace**; thou shalt be buried in a good old age'.

The use of the word here implies both safety and security.

Synonyms

Peace is a term of general application, and more comprehensive in meaning than quiet, calm, or tranquillity. It respects either communities or individuals; but quiet respects only individuals or small communities. Nations are said to have peace, but not quiet. Persons or families may have both peace and quiet. Peace implies an exemption from public or private strife; quiet implies a freedom from noise or interruption.

Peace and quiet, in regard to individuals, have likewise a reference to the internal state of the mind; but the former expresses the permanent condition of the mind, the latter its transitory condition.

Serious matters only can disturb our peace; trivial matters may disturb our quiet.

A good man enjoys the peace of a good conscience; but he may have unavoidable cares and anxieties which disturb his quiet.

Calm is a species of quiet, which respects objects in the natural or the moral world; it indicates the absence of violent motion, as well as violent noise; it is that state which more immediately succeeds a state of agitation.

Tranquillity, on the other hand, is taken more

absolutely; it expresses the situation as it exists in the present moment independently of what goes before or after: it is sometimes applicable to society, sometimes to natural objects, and sometimes to the mind.

Peace, as far as this world is concerned is, at its best, a pause between wars.

Illustrations from the Scriptures

Romans 5:1 is a conclusion following the treatise in the preceding chapters. After having proved that the whole world, including the Jew, is under sin, and under the hammer blow of God's judgment, the glorious light of the Gospel of the grace of God appears, whereby we may be declared not guilty, having a new standing before God. Such a salvation can only produce peace, in the sense of security and safety.

Colossians 1:20 declares the source of peace. It is through the instrumentality of the cross: and to make that point quite sure, it is the blood of His cross. Blood, in the Scripture, always means death applied. There is no peace to the heart that will not surrender to Him.

Perish

First mention

Genesis 41:36 'And that food shall be for store to the land against the seven years of famine, which shall be in the land of Egypt; that the land **perish** not through the famine.'

The word, in this context, cannot possibly mean complete and total annihilation, as the world would like to believe. Here, the word means that the land has been rendered useless by the famine, it has lost its function, but it still exists. So man, in his unbelief, shall perish, in the sense he will have lost his usefulness, and function, yet still exist q.v. eternal death and the end of Luke 15, coupled with the narrative of the rich man and Lazarus—dead, yet alive.

Synonyms
To perish expresses more than to die, and is applicable to many things. That which perishes does not always die. For instance, rubber may perish, but it does not die. But unregenerate man will die, and also perish, in the sense that rubber may perish, i.e. he has lost his usefulness.

To perish expresses the end (in the sense already given). Decay is the process by which this end is brought about. Something may be long in decaying, but when it perishes it ceases to be of any use.

Illustrations from the Scriptures
Luke 5:37 relates the parable of the vine and the bottles. The perishing of the old bottles implies that they still exist, but they have lost their usefulness.

Luke 15:17 relates the confession of the prodigal son when he came to himself: 'I perish with hunger'. He had realised that his life had lost its usefulness, and therefore it was time to repent.

Power

First mention
Exodus 9:16 'And in very deed for this cause have I raised thee up, for to shew in thee my **power**; and that

my name may be declared throughout all the earth'.

The power of God is spoken of here in connection with the sovereignty of God, and the fact that God is using His own enemy to display His power. The display of the power of God is also closely connected with the declaration of the name of God throughout all the earth. It is useful to compare this verse with Romans 9:17, where it is quoted in connection with the sovereignty of God.

Synonyms

Strength depends upon internal circumstances; power depends upon the external. Thus, a man may have strength to move, but not the power if he be bound with cords. Our strength is proportioned to the health of the body; our power may be increased by the help of some external means.

Subjects have sometimes the power of overturning the government, but they can in no case have the authority. Power may be abused; authority may be exceeded. Power may exist independently of right; authority is founded only on right.

A usurper has an assumed or usurped power; it is, therefore, exercised by no authority. The sovereign holds his power by the law of God; for God is the source of all authority, which is commensurate with His goodness, His power, and His wisdom. Man, therefore, exercises the supreme authority over man, as the minister of God's authority. He exceeds that authority if he does anything contrary to God's will.

Subjects have a delegated authority which they receive from a superior; if they act for themselves without respect to the will of that superior, they exert a power without authority. A minister of the gospel performs his functions by the authority of the gospel, but the power is not his own, it is the power of God.

It lies properly with the supreme power to grant privileges, or take them away; but the same may be done by one in whom the authority is invested.

Power is indefinite as to degree; one may have little or much power. Dominion is a positive degree of power.

Illustrations from the Scriptures

Romans 1:16 declares that the Gospel of Christ is the power of God unto salvation. The fact of the matter is that God is able to do for us that which we cannot do for ourselves. We are guilty sinners, condemned to die. Chapters 1, 2 and 3 show that we have no defence, and that every mouth is stopped. The order in this epistle is striking. Redemption by blood, and then redemption by power. 3:25 and 5:9 declare the first. Chapters 6, 7 and 8 declare the second. It is in keeping with the type in Exodus. Israel was delivered from Egypt and its bondage. It was redemption by blood, and then by power, and their deliverance was not complete until they stood on the wilderness side of the sea.

Praise

First mention

Genesis 29:35 'And she conceived again, and bare a son: and she said, Now will I **praise** the LORD: therefore she called his name Judah; and left bearing.'

PRAISE

In the text it states that the Lord opened the womb of Leah, and she bore four sons, and then left bearing. But the kindness and the grace of the Lord brought forth her praises. Therefore we conclude that praise is linked with the mighty acts that the Lord is able to perform.

Synonyms

The word 'praise' comes from the German '*preisen*', to value, and is akin to the English word 'price'. Therefore it signifies the giving of a value to a thing. The word 'commend' signifies to commit to the good opinion of others, whilst the word 'extol' signifies to lift up very high.

All these terms denote the act of expressing approbation. Praise is a general term. We praise generally, but commend particularly. We praise in stronger terms than we commend. To extol is to praise in strong terms. God, who expects our praise, will not be contented with simple commendation.

Illustrations from the Scriptures

Luke 18:43. The preceding verses tell the story of the blind beggar who received his sight. Please note that it was the people who witnessed this miracle that praised God. We can praise God for that which He has done for us, as individual believers; but we can also praise God for that which He has done for others. Both ways, God is praised, and that is how it must be.

'The praise of His glory' is a phrase that is used three times in the opening chapter of the epistle to the Ephesians. It helps divide the chapter into three sections. The first dealing with the work of God, the second dealing with the work of Christ, and the third dealing with the work of the Holy Spirit. The three phrases are to be found in verses 6, 12, and 14, and mark the end of each section.

Prayer

First mention
Genesis 20:7 'Now therefore restore the man his wife; for he is a prophet, and he shall **pray** for thee, and thou shalt live: and if thou restore her not, know thou that thou shalt surely die, thou, and all that are thine'.

A very important point is raised here. Remember that God is speaking here and could have preserved the life of Abimelech, and his family, without the intervention of prayer. But by prayer it had to be; and this is the way it has always been. God loves to hear a response from His people. We see prayer as not only asking when in need, but as communion with God—engaging in holy conversation.

Abraham is not praying for himself here, but for another, teaching us that our prayers should not be selfish.

Synonyms
Whilst prayer is a general term, there are other words that are more specific in their application:

1 Timothy 2:1 conveniently summarizes four of these words:
a. supplications (implying a need)
b. prayers (a general word)
c. intercessions (implying a petition)

d. giving of thanks (implying gratitude)

1 John 5:15 uses the word ask (implying begging, for we are all spiritual beggars, in the sense that God only can supply our need).

Illustrations from the Scriptures

The important question is: Why did Christ need to pray? To Him it was engaging in regular holy conversation with His Father in heaven. So it must for us—not coming to God in prayer only in the hour of need, but always practising His presence.

Genesis 32 teaches us that praying is laying hold on God. Its product is God laying hold on us.

Think not that we are able to change the mind of God when engaging in prayer. On the contrary, it is God that changes our mind to His way of thinking when we engage in prayer. Luke 11 repays careful study because it teaches us many things about prayer. The Lord did not have to teach His disciples how to pray, but what to pray FOR.

The following points emerge from the reading:
a. God's interests first.
b. spiritual needs more important than temporal needs.
c. prayers are not to be selfish—'give us'.
d. not to pray for useless things.
e. not to pray for harmful things.

In Ephesians 6 we learn that the Roman soldier had 6 parts to his armour. The believer has seven. The seventh being prayer, as in verses 18 and 19.

Priest

First mention

Genesis 14:18 'And Melchizedek king of Salem brought forth bread and wine; and he was the **priest** of the most high God.'

It is important to compare this verse with the reference to the self-same person in Hebrews 5:6 which reads: 'Thou art a priest for ever after the order of Melchizedek'. The writer of the epistle found the truth of priesthood hard to teach (read verses 11 to 14 in chapter 5). To the Jewish mind the idea of atonement was inseparable from the function of the priest. The teaching in this epistle is that the priesthood of Christ is based on the atonement perfected (Hebrews 1:3). To make Christ a priest for ever presenting a sacrifice would be to discredit the efficacy of the cross. The burden of this epistle is found in the phrase 'once for all'. Verse 5 in chapter 5 refers to His resurrection and NOT His birth, remembering that the epistle commences at Exodus 24, and NOT Exodus 12. In Exodus 24, Moses is seen as a type of Christ, ascending to the mountain, and after a time descending with the pattern for the tabernacle. Then, and then only, does the priesthood begin. So Christ rose again from the dead, ascending to His Father on high, is now our High Priest in heaven. Hebrews 3:14 'passed into the heavens'. We have an high priest that can be touched with the feeling of our infirmities. Hebrews 6:20 'Whither the forerunner is for us entered, even Jesus', and here, once again, Melchizedek is mentioned. Hebrews 7:25, once again in the context of Melchizedek, declares 'seeing He ever liveth to make intercession for them'.

PRIEST

The Bible becomes its own commentary. The epistle to the Hebrews defines clearly the function of the priest.

Synonyms

As the reader may have already discovered, much of the information in this section has been drawn from secular sources. Much confusion and error exists in the definition of a priest. The word is invariably linked with such terms as 'clergy', 'parson', and 'minister'. The 'popular' meaning of the word is that person who holds the sacredotal office. This is a sharp lesson never to refer to secular dictionaries for the meaning of words in the Scriptures. The Bible is its own commentary, and it incorporates its own dictionary and lexicon.

Illustrations from the Scriptures

Hebrews 4:14. The priest out of office was called the 'great priest', whilst the priest in office was called the 'high priest'. At the trial of Christ two names are mentioned: Annas and Caiaphas (John 18:13). Presumably Annas was the 'great priest', and Caiaphas was the 'high priest' (the latter is definitely stated). It was impossible for any one man to be the great high priest—EXCEPT CHRIST!

Hebrews 2:17 'to make reconciliation for the sins of the people'. Christ's priestly work is NOT to justify and sanctify (i.e. the removing of the guilt and the defilement of sin respectively). This was secured at Calvary, and depended on the shed blood of Christ. Christ's priestly work is stated in this verse under consideration. Reconciliation FOLLOWS redemption, and removes the estrangement that sin produces.

Promise

First mention

Exodus 12:25 'And it shall come to pass, when ye be come to the land which the LORD will give you, according as he hath **promised**, that ye shall keep this service'.

The promise is linked with the following points:
a. A certainty: 'when' not 'if' ye come to the land.
b. The LORD, i.e. Jehovah, the covenant keeping God. The God who makes the promises, and keeps them.
c. 'Which the LORD will give you'. It was a gift by the grace of God.
d. 'That ye shall keep this service'. The promise is linked to the Passover, and therefore to redemption by blood.

Thus we learn that our salvation depends on the promises of God: a salvation that rests on the finished work of Christ, who is our Passover.

Synonyms

Promise is compounded from two Latin words that mean to fix beforehand.

The promise is specific, and consequently more binding than the engagement. A promise is linked with the recipient's faith in the word of the giver. As a promise and engagement can be made only by word, the word is often put for either or for both. Thus, we have already learnt that faith is taking God at His Word (Romans 10:17). His Word is another way of expressing the promises of God, and our salvation depends on the promises of God, as already stated.

Illustrations from the Scriptures

2 Corinthians 1:20 declares that all the promises of God in Him (i.e. Christ) are yea, and in Him Amen. This means that all the promises of God are fulfilled in Christ, His Son. The preceding verse amplifies this point in talking about the way in which Christ was preached. There was no variableness or inconstancy or inconsistency—always one and the same, centring in Him.

Galatians chapter 3 in dealing with the function of the law, talks much of the promise of God. Thus in verse 16 we learn that the fulfilment of the promise to Abraham was reserved for the Messianic dispensation. The law was ushered in between the giving of the promise and its fulfilment. **The law came later than the promise, and could not alter the terms of its fulfilment.** In verse 17 we further learn that God ratified the covenant with Abraham, which the law could not annul, being brought into operation 430 years later. The gift was bestowed by promise, and not by obedience to the law. This chapter repays careful study on this point, and the function of the law.

Prophecy

First mention

Genesis 20:7 'Now therefore restore the man his wife; for he is a **prophet**, and he shall pray for thee, and thou shalt live: and if thou restore her not, know that thou shalt surely die, thou, and all that are thine'.

An unfortunate incident in which God had to overrule. God promised to Abraham a seed that would be as numberless as the stars (chapter 15). But Sarah was barren, Abraham tried to take a short cut and thus Ishmael was born of the bondwoman Hagar (chapter 16 and compare with Galatians chapter 4). The fulfilment of the promise of God does not occur until chapter 21, when Isaac was born of Sarah, even after her time of life. Chapter 20, and the verse under consideration, occur between these two events. 'Restore the man his wife' was necessary in the light of the coming birth of Isaac, the son of promise, NOT the son of the flesh.

Abraham is called a prophet here in the sense that he has insight (go back to the revelation in chapter 15), and that he forth tells (as opposed to foretelling) present truth in the light of the future.

Thus to summarize:

prophecy can be: backsight
                  insight
                  foresight.

The prophet can: foretell the future in the light of the present.
                  forth tell the present in the light of the future.

The teacher can give: present truth in the light of the past.

Synonyms

Once again the definitions in secular literature rather let us down here, because they only suggest the meaning of foretelling and prediction. The Bible must be its own interpreter here; nothing else will do.

We speak of a prediction being verified, and a prophecy

being fulfilled. To prognosticate is an act of the understanding.

Illustrations from the Scriptures
Going back to Abraham, and Genesis chapter 18, we learn that Abraham has a glimpse into the future, and the ultimate destruction of the cities of the plain. Abraham does not use the information to speculate, but to intercede on the behalf of any who may be found righteous in those cities.

In terms of Daniel 2,7,8,9 and on to the end of the book, Matthew 24, Ezekiel 37, 38, and 39, Zechariah 14, and almost the entire book of Revelation, we have many glimpses into the future. We must not speculate upon these things, but rather sink to our knees and pray for the lost, who do not know the fate that awaits them.

Propitiation

First mention
Excluding its Old Testament connections, which will be discussed later on, the first mention of the word, as such, is not until Romans 3:25.

'Whom God hath set forth to be a **propitiation** through faith in His blood, to declare His righteousness for the remission of sins that are past, through the forebearance of God.'

The word is linked with: man's faith
Christ's blood
God's righteousness.

When we speak of the blood of Christ, we must turn

back to the Old Testament and the types to see the meaning of the blood. The word 'propitiation' brings to mind the mercy seat of the tabernacle, situated in the holy place. Once a year the high priest could enter and that not without blood. Thus those sacrifices in the Old Testament pointed on to the one great eternal sacrifice—the death of Christ, and the shedding of His most precious blood. Those sins of the old testament were not ignored, and God did not condone them. But time waited for the first advent of Christ and His death upon the cross. Thus God maintains His righteous integrity.

Synonyms

'Favourable' properly characterizes both persons and things; that which is propitious characterizes the person only. An equal may be favourable; a superior only is propitious.

Auspicious, unlike favourable, is only applicable to things.

Illustrations from the Scriptures

Although the word, as such, is not employed in Luke 18:13, the thought is exactly the same. The publican was asking God to look upon him, as He looked upon the mercy seat of the tabernacle. Look in favour upon me—but this would be impossible without blood, and that the blood of Christ.

We must be careful today not to be guilty of preaching an anaemic gospel, i.e. a gospel that dispenses with the preaching of the blood of Christ.

Ransom

First mention

Exodus 21:30 'If there be laid on him a sum of money, then he shall give for the **ransom** of his life whatsoever is laid upon him'.

The word is closely linked with a price to be paid, and the matter of life, as opposed to death. It is the ransom of his life; a price put on the value of a life.

Synonyms

The ransom is the price of redemption. The basic meaning is the transfer of ownership from one to another through the payment of a price or an equivalent substitute.

Both persons and things can be redeemed, but only persons are ransomed. Redeem takes into account both deliverance from bondage, and the price necessary to bring this about. Ransom takes into account the price paid only.

Illustrations from the Scriptures

It is used of:
a. the redemption of a slave girl for marriage.
b. the redemption of a man's life under sentence of death.
c. redemption of Israel from Egypt, by the slaughter of the firstborn.
d. deliverance from danger by the Psalmist.

Mark 10:45 is a well known verse that puts the word into perspective. Ransom is linked with a price that was too high for man to pay. The Lord Jesus Christ laid down His life. To us, salvation is free, because we cannot pay the price.

To whom or what this price was paid, we do not know. Any suggestions would be conjecture only.

'None of the ransomed ever knew how deep were the waters crossed'.

Reconciliation

First mention

Leviticus 6:30 'And no sin offering, whereof any of the blood is brought into the tabernacle of the congregation to **reconcile** withal in the holy place, shall be eaten: it shall be burnt in the fire'.

The word is closely linked with the shedding and the application of blood, as well as sin. The context concerns the law of the sin offering and embraces the following sins and the estrangement produced thereby:

a. **Ecclesiastical sins** —the priest
b. **National sins** —the people
c. **Administrative sins** —the public servant
d. **Personal sins** —the private individual

Synonyms

Conciliate and reconcile are both employed in the sense of uniting men's affections, but under different circumstances.

The conciliator gets the good-will and affections for himself; the reconciler unites the affections of two parties to each other. The conciliator may either gain new affections, or regain those which are lost; the reconciler always renews affections which have once been lost.

Men in power have sometimes the happy opportunity of conciliating the good-will of those who are most adverse to their authority, and thus reconciling them to measures which would otherwise be odious.

'It must be confessed a happy attachment, which can reconcile the Laplander to his freezing snows, and the African to his scorching sun'—Cumberland.

Illustrations from the Scriptures

Ephesians 2:13 declares that we have been made 'nigh by the blood, for He is our peace'. Reconciliation, therefore, is a step beyond redemption, and is the fulfilment of redemption. The cross was the work **of** Christ, but it was a work **for** God. God is the Peace maker and has reconciled us to Himself; therefore let us know the peace of it in our hearts.

Romans 5:6 to 11 repay careful study in connection with the meaning of reconciliation. Thus we learn that we were without strength, and therefore incapable of working out any righteousness for ourselves; and in such a state Christ died for the ungodly—not a distinct class, but mankind in general. God gives adequate proof of His love towards us, in that even when we were the declared enemies of God, Christ died on our behalf. The shedding of the blood of Christ was essential for the removal of the guilt of sin, hence we are justified. Verse 10 declares that reconciliation is a step beyond redemption. This is the divine order—there must be the shedding of blood first. Verse 11 uses the word 'atonement', which is better translated by the word 'reconciliation'. What we have here is the EFFECTS of the atonement.

Redemption

First mention
Exodus 6:6 'Wherefore say unto the children of Israel, I am the LORD, and I will bring you out from under the burdens of the Egyptians, and I will rid you out of their bondage, and I will **redeem** you with a stretched out arm, and with great judgments'.

This reference does not ignore that, in Genesis 48:16, where an angel is referred to. Here it speaks of the redemption which is of God.

In the verse under consideration, redemption is linked with the burdens and the bondage of Egypt, and with the promise of deliverance from them. Later in the book it is to be seen that there could be no redemption without the shedding and the application of blood. After that it can be seen that redemption is by power, and over the Red Sea into the wilderness.

Synonyms
Compare with the remarks on the word 'ransom'. The ransom, we learnt, is the price that was paid for redemption. The two words are linked. But redemption also has in it the thought of deliverance, as we have already seen in Exodus 6:6. Therefore it does not only refer to the cost, but the actual deliverance from bondage.

Illustrations from the Scriptures
Several New Testament passages put redemption into perspective.

Romans 3:25 teaches that our redemption in Christ was instrumental in our justification; the shedding of blood that removed the guilt of sin.

Romans 8:23 talks of the redemption of our body as something yet future, as well as a redemption that is past as seen in Romans 3.

Ephesians 1:7 links redemption with the blood of Christ, whereas Ephesians 4:30, looking to the future, declares that we are sealed by the Spirit unto the day of redemption, i.e. the coming of Christ for His church. That sealing is the sign of security, ownership and guarantee.

Hebrews 9:12 defines our redemption as being eternal. This involves more than time, it includes a quality that transcends anything that the world may offer.

Regeneration

First mention
Matthew 19:28 'And Jesus said unto them, Verily I say unto you, That ye which have followed me, in the **regeneration** when the Son of Man shall sit in the throne of His glory, ye also shall sit upon twelve thrones, judging the twelve tribes of Israel'.

In considering regeneration here, (alias the new birth in connection with the Kingdom of God) the first mention of the word, in question, is in a book that has as its theme the Kingdom of heaven, and the title used of the Lord is the Son of Man. The word 'of' in the title Son of Man is employed in the sense of being superior over, as in the title King of kings, and Lord of lords.

Here, the context has in mind the spiritual (not the national or political) rebirth of the nation of Israel.

Synonyms

Regeneration stresses the new as opposed to the old, whilst new birth stresses spiritual life as opposed to spiritual death. Whilst new birth and regeneration are not successive stages, regeneration and renewal **are** (see Titus 3:5). Renewal implies a change all over and represents the subsequent work of the Holy Spirit in our lives after regeneration.

Illustrations from the Scriptures

The mind readily turns to John 3, when thinking of this subject; but the relevant verses need careful examination. Baptismal regeneration is not taught here—it has no place in Scripture. The verses in question do not refer to baptism as such, for how could Nicodemus have heard of the believer's baptism? This would be a glaring anachronism.

If the word 'and' in verse 5 is taken to mean 'even', then the water makes reference to the Spirit of God. But if the word 'and' is simply read as a conjunction, then the water makes reference to the Word of God (see 1 Peter 1:23).

Remission

First mention
Matthew 26:28 'For this is my blood of the new testament, which is shed for many for the **remission** of sins'.

The word is closely linked with sin, and its removal, and the shedding of the blood of Christ, the price that had to be paid.

Synonyms
Compare with the word 'forgive', and 'pardon' in this book.

The pardon of sin obliterates that which is past and restores the sinner to the Divine favour; it is promised throughout Scripture to all men on the condition of faith and repentance: remission of sin alone averts the Divine vengeance, which otherwise would fall upon those who are guilty of it; and it is granted to all believers on the ground of Christ's death, and the shedding of His most precious blood.

Illustrations from the Scriptures
The word, as such, does not occur in the Old Testament, so we have to look to the New Testament for illustrations of the word.

Romans 3:25 God, here, maintains His righteous integrity in dealing with former sins. The cross of Christ stands in the centre of the history of mankind as a monument to the grace of God, dwarfing the achievements of man at his best. God has set forth Christ to declare and vindicate His own righteousness. Forgiveness is the work of grace, but here, remission is the work of

Repentance

First mention
Genesis 6:6 'And it **repented** the LORD that He had made man on the earth, and it grieved Him at His heart'.

The most surprising feature of this first mention of the word 'repentance' is that it concerns God, not man! It does not make man any better; in fact, it makes him worse. The context shows that the wickedness of man was great, and that God would have destroyed every living creature, both man and beast. The root behind the word is that of change of heart and mind. Even though man was so wicked, grace was there (verse 8), and not as an afterthought either!

Synonyms
Penitence signifies simply sorrow for what is amiss. Contrition, derived from a Latin verb to rub together, means to bruise, as it were with sorrow. Compunction signifies to prick thoroughly, and remorse signifies to have a gnawing pain.

All these terms express sorrow in one way or another, but repentance expresses more than sorrow, it reflects a change of heart and mind.

Illustrations from the Scriptures
Mark 1:15 links repentance with faith in the gospel. They are not separate acts to be successively entered

into to gain salvation, but different phases of the same Godward attitude of the soul of man. There cannot be salvation without repentance, any more than without faith. Repentance is not faith, and faith is not repentance; yet they are inseparable, that is, in connection with the gospel.

Acts 3:19 connects repentance with conversion, indicating a change of direction. Acts 26:20 augments this thought and commands a turning to God.

In the letters to the seven churches in Revelation 2 and 3, repentance figures prominently. The preaching and teaching of repentance is not only confined to the gospel platform, but is needed on the ministry platform also.

Resurrection

First mention

Matthew 22:23 'The same day came to Him the Sadducees, which say that there is no **resurrection**, and asked Him,'

Although the first mention of the word is in the New Testament, the doctrine of the resurrection takes us back to Abraham (Genesis 22) and the patriarch Job (Job 19:25).

Although it may seem strange, the first mention of the word refers to a disbelief in this fundamental truth. Compare this with the argument that Paul uses in 1 Corinthians 15, where he assumes, at first, that there is no resurrection and therefore proves that the resurrection is true beyond any shadow of doubt.

Synonyms

'Rise again,' 'rise up from the dead,' and 'quicken' are all employed in this great theme. The basic meaning of the word is 'to cause to stand up'. Those that were raised from the dead, as recorded in Scripture as miracles, did die later, to await the ultimate resurrection from the dead. But Revelation 1:18 makes it perfectly clear with respect to the resurrection of Christ; 'I am He that liveth, and was dead; and, behold I am alive for evermore, Amen'.

Illustrations from the Scriptures

1 Corinthians 15 is a prominent and important passage on this subject.

Verses 3 and 4 represent the Gospel in a nutshell, emphasising three salient features: His death, His burial, and His resurrection. Please note that it is important to preach the burial of Christ, because it defines His death—He did die (not swooned according to one theory). But what is more to the point here, the burial defines the resurrection—it was a physical resurrection (not a spiritual resurrection as some would limit it).

Righteousness

First mention

Genesis 7:1 'And the LORD said unto Noah, Come thou and all thy house into the ark; for thee have I seen **righteous** before Me in this generation'.

The word, here, is closely linked with God and that

RIGHTEOUSNESS

which He sees, and it is set in contrast to the wicked and evil generation that God destroyed. It is that quality that God requires in a man. Later we shall see that man has no righteousness of his own that can fit him for heaven.

Synonyms

Righteous signifies conformable to right and truth, and is a contraction of the old English word 'rightwise', i.e. going the right way. Godly is a contraction of Godlike. These epithets are both used in a spiritual sense, and cannot be introduced into any other discourse than that which is properly spiritual. Godliness, in the strict sense, is that outward deportment which characterizes a heavenly temper, such as prayer, reading of the Scriptures, and worship. Righteousness on the other hand comprehends Christian morality, as distinct from any such thing that apertains to the heathen or the unbeliever. A righteous man does right, not only because it is right, but because it is agreeable to the will of God.

Illustrations from the Scriptures

Two terms must be defined and distinguished in the Scriptures.

Romans 1:17 'The righteousness of God'.

Philippians 3:9 'The righteousness which is of God by faith'.

The first is talking about the integrity and the character of God. In fact the entire epistle deals with the righteousness of God in different aspects:

1. The righteousness of God in relation to sin 1:16 to 3:20.
2. The righteousness of God in relation to salvation 3:21 to 5:21.

3. The righteousness of God in relation to sanctification 6:1 to 8:39.
4. The righteousness of God in relation to the sovereignty of God 9:1 to 11:36.
5. The righteousness of God in relation to service 12:1 to the end.

The second term is talking about that righteousness which is imputed, or reckoned to us through the instrumentality of faith. Look up the word justification, and Genesis 15:6, the first reference to the imputation of righteousness. We have no righteousness of our own in the sight of God (in the sight of man, yes, but it is with God that we have to deal). It is a standing before God, that afterwards has to be 'lived down' by practical sanctification. Mind you, we **are** sanctified, but we have to realise it and live it out.

Salvation

First mention
Genesis 12:12 'Therefore it shall come to pass, when the Egyptians shall see thee, that they shall say, This is his wife: and they will kill me, but they will **save** thee alive'.

Admittedly this reference does not speak of the salvation of the Lord, but it does give us the root meaning of the word, i.e. to preserve life, to avoid destruction.

Synonyms
Deliver signifies to make free; rescue signifies by

SALVATION

succour to get one out of a difficulty; save signifies to make safe and secure.

The idea of taking or keeping from danger is common to these terms; but deliver and rescue signify rather to take from; save, to keep from danger. Deliver and rescue do not necessarily convey the idea of the means by which the end is produced; save includes the idea of a superior agency.

To rescue is a species of delivering, namely delivering from the power of another; to save is applicable to the greatest possible evils. A person may be delivered from a burden, from an oppression, from disease, or from danger; a prisoner is rescued from the hands of an enemy, but a person is saved from destruction.

Spare signifies to free; preserve signifies to keep off; protect signifies to defend.

The idea of keeping from evil is the common idea of all these terms, and the peculiar significance of the term save.

They differ either in the nature of the evil kept off, or the circumstances of the agent. We may be saved from every kind of evil; but we are spared only from that which it is in the power of another to inflict. We may be saved from falling, or saved from an illness; a criminal is spared from punishment.

We are preserved and protected from evils of magnitude; thus we are preserved from ruin or protected from oppression.

Thus the idea of the term under consideration is twofold, as is confirmed by the Word of God:

a. security —in order to stop the enemy, Satan, from getting in.

b. separation —saved from the present evil age, and thus separated unto God.

Illustrations from the Scriptures

The subject of salvation is a vast one that embraces so many truths, and words that are discussed between the covers of this book:

Regeneration	a change of nature
Redemption	a change of ownership
Repentance	a change of heart and mind
Forgiveness	a change of circumstances
Conversion	a change of direction
Justification	a change of state
Hope	a change of prospects
Adoption	a change of family

Ephesians 2:8 explains that salvation is the gift of God; it is given by grace, and received by faith. It is a gift because we cannot afford to pay the price, and that price was the shedding of the most precious blood of the Lord Jesus Christ as He died upon the cross.

Jude 22, 23 and 24 make reference to our great salvation in terms of not only security, but separation.

Verse 22 explains that some have to be dealt with carefully and lovingly; whilst verse 23 is the very opposite in pulling the soul in danger out of the fire in a drastic manner.

Verse 24 talks of our salvation in terms of preservation and the prospect of one day being in His presence.

Sanctification

First mention

Genesis 2:3 'And God blessed the seventh day, and **sanctified** it: because that in it He rested from all His work which God had created and made.'

Please note that the seventh day was different to the other six, and was separated from them, in as much as God rested on that day from all His work. Thus we have the root meaning of the word. It is that which is different, separated, and holy. If we claim to be a sanctified people, then we must live holy, separate lives, acting differently to the people of this world.

Synonyms

Holiness, which comes from the northern languages, has altogether acquired a Christian significance: it respects (in the context of our subject) the life and temper of a believer. Sanctification, a word of the same meaning as holiness, is derived from the Latin tongue.

Holiness is a thing not to be affected; it is that genuine characteristic of the believer which is altogether spiritual, and cannot be counterfeited.

Sanctity, on the other hand, is from its very nature exposed to falshood, and the least to be trusted; when it displays itself in individuals, either by the sorrowful look, or the singular cut of their garments, or other singularities of action and gesture, it is of the most questionable nature.

Sacred is less than holy; the sacred derives its sanction from human authorities, and is connected rather with our moral than our spiritual duties. That which is holy is altogether spiritual, and abstracted from the earthly.

Illustrations from the Scriptures

There can be much misconception about sanctification, which the Scriptures alone can clarify.

Sin produces guilt, defilement and estrangement. It is the defilement of sin that we are speaking about here in the subject of sanctification. Hebrews 13:12 declares 'He might sanctify the people with His own blood'. This is a lost truth today, i.e. that we are already sanctified by His blood, through the efficacy of the cross.

The tenses used of the Greek verb give us the clue about sanctification:

The present continuous tense is used in Greek as an expression of both the past and the future, and therefore in one sense there is such a thing as progressive sanctification.

Another tense used (the aorist) consider it as a past transaction, one definite act, not to be repeated—at the cross. We are sanctified and we have to enter into the realisation of it. (Study Romans 6,7 and 8).

Another tense used is the perfect tense, which has the force of something that happened in the past, which we can enjoy in the present.

The religionist tries to be what he cannot be.

The redeemed has to realise what he already is.

A separate treatise on this vital subject is given here, tracing the course of the word through both the New Testament and the Old Testament.

Sanctification
Its course through OT and NT

The Old Testament
First mention
Genesis 2:3 'blessed the seventh day and **sanctified** it'. One of the seven, yet different, discrete, separate, set apart, ordered by God, and given by God

used of things Lev. 8:11 '**sanctify them**' i.e. altar, vessels, laver.

used of persons Lev. 8:12 '**sanctify him**'.

used of places Exod. 19:23 'And Moses said unto the Lord, The people come up to the mount Sinai: for thou chargest us, saying, Set bounds about the mount and **sanctify it**.

Lev. 11:44-47 (Its meaning discovered by its use).

v.44 establishes His name and character.

'**yourselves**' embraces all

'**sanctify yourselves**' active participation—not only passive.

'**shall be holy**' future and progressive.

'**I am holy**' the motive and aim.

'**defile**' sin brings guilt and defilement. Removal of guilt by justification (q.v. Romans 3 and 4). Removal of defilement by **sanctification** (q.v. Romans 6 to 8). This is the divine order. Redemption by blood, and then by power. Burnt offering THEN the meal offering.

v.45 reminded of their deliverance. Progress from there. '**Be holy**' Egypt MUST be taken out. Hence exodus, new calendar, and divine demonstration against the gods of Egypt.

v.47 'to make a difference' the root meaning of the word.

Hebrew word for = *qâdash* = belonging to the sphere of the holy, as distinct from the common or profane. Probably from root 'to separate' as in the place Kadesh Barnea.

translated hallow, holy, sanctify, consecrate, dedicate. The book of Leviticus repays careful study on this subject and an outline of the book is available.

The New Testament

Greek words used *hagiazō* = I separate, consecrate, cleanse, purify from the root *hagios* = separate from the common condition. Originally used of devotion to the Greek mythological gods.

hoi Hagioi = saints or holy ones and is the usual, ordinary name for the saved. 'Christian' was a nickname, as other names down through the history of the church q.v. 1 Cor 1:2 **'called saints'** NOT 'called to be saints' i.e. constituted saints by the call of God. *klētois* = an adjective qualifying the noun NOT a verb.

How the verb is used

Active voice (the agent)

present tense	I sanctify
aorist tense	I sanctified

Passive (the object)

present tense	I am being sanctified
aorist tense	I am sanctified
perfect tense	I have been sanctified.

SANCTIFICATION

Sanctification to us the object is
1. **Continuous** the present tense, also used in Greek as an expression of the past and the future.
2. **Complete** the aorist tense, a past transaction, one definite act, not to be repeated, once for all.
3. **Cultivated** the perfect tense in the past with the effects in the present. A realisation in the present of something in the past.

---

1. **Continuous** as used in the present tense with links with both the past and the future. A constant conformity to a standard. Present tense used of God who sanctifies. q.v. *Jahweh* = 'I am' = Jehovah = an incomplete action in Hebrew = the continuing God. Present tense used of the believer who is sanctified.
Heb. 2:11 'He that **sanctifieth** and they who are **sanctified** are all one: for which cause He is not ashamed to call them brethren'. Both verbs are in the present tense. V.10 talks about a continuing God.
Heb. 10:14 'By one offering He hath perfected for ever them that are **sanctified**'.
1 Tim. 4:5 'For it is **sanctified** by the word of God and prayer' referring to every creature of God.

2. **Complete** as used in the aorist tense—a past transaction—a momentary action—one definite act—not to be repeated—once for all. Not to be undone ('I smashed the plate'—'I crashed the car'—'I burnt the paper') Holiness has no degree: either holy or unholy; either clean or unclean NOT LESS HOLY. (q.v. the book of Leviticus and its teaching).

1 Cor. 1:30 'made unto us **sanctification**' 'is made' = *egenēthē* = aorist tense of *ginomai* = become.
John 17:17 '**sanctify** them through thy truth' = in the truth.
1 Cor. 6:11 '**sanctified** in the name of the Lord Jesus, and by the Spirit of our God'.
Eph. 5:26 'That He might **sanctify** and cleanse it with the washing of water by the word' lit. 'in order that it, He might sanctify—cleansing by the washing of the water by word' (+ *rhēmati* = spoken word)
1 Thess. 5:23 'And the very God of peace **sanctify** you wholly; and I pray God your whole spirit and sould and body be preserved blameless unto the coming of our Lord Jesus Christ' 'I pray God' not in the Greek MS and 'and' should read 'even' now reads: 'And Himself the God of peace may **sanctify** you complete, even your entire spirit and soul and body' 'wholly' refers to the completeness of man NOT the process of **sanctification**.
Heb. 13:12 'He might sanctify the people with His own blood' **Sanctification** by blood—a lost truth today. NOT used as a progressive stage here, but as complete.
1 Pet. 3:15 'But **sanctify** the Lord God in your hearts' lit. 'but as Lord, the Christ **sanctify** in your hearts'. 'Here in the active voice and not the passive voice. i.e. I make Christ separate and different to anything else in my life, hence He is Lord.

3. **Cultivated** as used in the perfect tense, with its effects in the present q.v. John 19:30 *tetelestai* = 'It is finished' q.v. 1 Cor 15:20 *egēgertai* = 'is Christ risen'. Here it is the realisation of these things in the present.

The religionist trying to become what he is not.
The redeemed trying to realise what he is.
'Saints and sinners' is a false antithesis. Every saint is a sinner—though not every sinner is a saint.
John 17:19 'I sanctify myself, that they also might be **sanctified** through the truth' lit. 'having been **sanctified** in truth' i.e. truth NOT falsehood, reality NOT shadow, complete NOT incomplete. 'I sanctify myself' is an assertion of His deity.
Acts 20:32 'an inheritance among all them which are **sanctified**'.
Rom. 15:16 '**sanctified** by the Holy Ghost' no definite article, stressing the operation of the Spirit.
1 Cor. 1:2 '**sanctified** in Christ Jesus'.
2 Tim. 2:21 '**sanctified** meet for the Master's use'.
Heb. 10:10 'by the which will we are **sanctified** through the offering of the body of Jesus Christ, once for all'

Summary

We are **sanctified** by   God the Father
the Spirit
the name of the Lord Jesus
in Christ Jesus
by the blood of Christ
by the word of God.

God is the author
The Spirit is the agent   of our **sanctification**
The blood the means
and it is in Christ that this is ours, and the Word of God testifies to this.

It is not automatic—we cannot 'continue in sin, that grace may abound' (Romans). We are declared 'not guilty' (justification Romans 3 to 5) and we must live it down (sanctification Romans 6 to 8). It is the realisation of it that we must attain.

Separation

First mention
Genesis 13:9 'Is not the whole land before thee? **separate** thyself, I pray thee from me: if thou wilt take the left hand, then I will go to the right; or if thou depart to the right hand, then I will go to the left'.

This verse and verse 11 indicate the parting of the ways for Abraham and Lot. The word involves separation to, and separation from, as implied by this incident. For Lot, the choice was disastrous, in as much as he went into Sodom, and then Sodom was in him. So it is today: to go into the world will eventually mean the world getting into us.

Synonyms
Abstracted signifies to turn aside from the object that is present. For instance a man can be abstracted from all the surrounding scenes: his senses are locked up from all the objects that seek for admittance.

Distinguish signifies to give different marks to things, by which they may be known from each other. Thus we distinguish that which we do not wish to confound.

Discrete derives from the Latin to sift, and denotes that which is individually distinct.

Isolate and insulate derive from the Latin for an island, and in particular, isolate denotes to place apart or alone.

Separation is NOT isolation, and the thought behind the word is closely connected with sanctification (q.v.). If you recall the reference in Genesis 2:3, the seventh day was one of the seven, yet it was different. So separation; we are in the world, but not of it.

Illustrations from the Scriptures

Romans 1:1 teaches us that it is a work of God, being separated unto the Gospel of God. Matthew 13:49 declares that there is a separation in Divine judgment in the context of the truths concerning the Kingdom of Heaven.

2 Corinthians 6:17 teaches separation of the believer from the unbeliever. The previous verses employ five different words to express five different areas of our lives where there must be separation:

a. Professional or business associations
 —Righteousness v. unrighteousness
b. Political or national associations
 —Light v. darkness
c. Marital associations
 —Christ v. Belial
d. Social associations
 —Believer v. unbeliever
e. Spiritual associations
 —Temple of God v. idols.

Sin

First mention

Genesis 4:7 'If thou doest well, shalt thou not be accepted? and if thou doest not well, **sin** lieth at the door. And unto thee shall be his desire, and thou shalt rule over him'.

We read of sin coming into this world in chapter 3 (which we will deal with later) but here is the first mention of the word. It seems that the text refers to an animal as being available at the door, i.e. a sin offering. Sin produces guilt, defilement and estrangement, but sin, in itself, is lawlessness. The way to be accepted of God must be by the shedding of blood. And here, as early as Genesis 4, the foundation is laid.

Synonyms

Crime signifies a judgment, sentence, or punishment; and also the cause of the sentence or punishment, in which latter sense it is here taken.

Vice, from the Latin to avoid, signifies that which ought to be avoided.

Sin, a Saxon word, derived from the Greek and then the Latin, a verb meaning to hurt, signifies the thing that hurts.

Crime is a social offence; vice is a personal offence: sin is an offence against God. Crime violates human laws; vice violates moral laws: sin violates the law of God. Therefore there are many sins which are not described as crimes or vices.

Crimes and vices are brought before human courts: sins are brought before the high court of God.

Crime and vice can go unpunished: sin carries its own punishment, and cannot escape the eye of God.

Crimes are particular acts; vices are habitual acts: sin is a way of life.

The punishment meted out for crimes and vices vary

from one country to another: the punishment of sin is unchangeable—it is death (Romans 6:23).

Illustrations from the Scriptures

Reverting to Genesis chapter 3, we see that sin is lawlessness, disobedience—a deliberate violation of the command of God. It was not so much that a bite was taken out of the forbidden fruit, but that a bite was taken out of the commandment of God. The permissive society began here, and, since Adam, man has turned prodigal.

Romans 3:23 affords an important clue with respect to the true meaning of sin, and how the Greek language expressed it. The word, as used in the New Testament, is derived from a greek word that literally means 'not to have a share'—and consequently came to mean a missing of the mark. This idea is expressed in Romans 3:23 in the phrase: 'come short of the glory of God'. The whole point of our existence is that we should live our lives to the glory of God. Anything short of this is sin. This point MUST be emphasised from the gospel platform; that the ordinary man in the street may realise he is a sinner and needs salvation through Christ.

As already stated, sin produces:
    guilt   the need is justification
    defilement   the need is sanctification
    estrangement the need is reconciliation.

Teach

First mention

Exodus 4:12 'Now therefore go, and I will be with thy mouth, and **teach** thee what thou shalt say'.

The word here possesses qualities that the secular meaning of the word does not enjoy.

a. There must be a commission from God, Himself.
b. There is the promise that God will be with the mouth that teaches.
c. Tt is God alone that teaches. That teaching today is accomplished through the Holy Spirit of God.

Synonyms

Inform, instruct, and teach are terms that are employed in the communication of knowledge, and this is the common idea which connects them.

To inform and to teach are employed for things as well as persons; to instruct only for persons: books and reading inform the mind; history or experience teaches mankind.

The word instruct (as employed in Philippians 4:12) is derived from a Greek verb that implies being initiated into a secret (q.v. the treatise on the word mystery).

Illustrations from the Scriptures

2 Timothy 4:3 warns of those with itching ears, i.e. ears that cannot be satisfied, employing teachers that only teach the things that they wish to hear. The teacher, today, needs to touch the heart, not tickle the ear.

John 3:2 records the confession of Nicodemus on that night that he met the Lord Jesus Christ: 'Thou art a teacher come from God'. The Lord Jesus Christ is the greatest of all teachers, and we can do no better than to follow Him.

a. He taught by contrast
b. He taught by comparison

c. He taught with conviction
d. He taught with compassion
e. He taught by His conduct.

Temptation

First mention

Genesis 22:1 'And it came to pass after these things, that God did **tempt** Abraham, and said unto him, Abraham: and he said, Behold, here I am'.

The word, here in this first reference, is a good example of the confusion that can result from the meaning of temptation and trial, or testing. We are going to see later on that temptations come from within and are to be resisted, whilst testing comes from God and is to be endured. The latter is the case here. The opening phrase of the verse refers to the previous chapter and the birth of the son of promise, Isaac. This is the supreme trial of Abraham's faith in order to show that God demands implicit obedience.

Synonyms

Trial is derived from the Hebrew to stretch, and signifies to stretch the power.

Tempt is derived from the Latin to stretch, and signifies to impel to action by efforts.

Allure is derived from the German meaning a tempting bait, and signifies to present something to please the senses.

Seduce is derived from the Latin to lead, and signifies to lead anyone aside.

Decoy is derived from the German for a cage for birds,

and signifies to draw into any place for the purpose of getting into one's power.

We try a person only in the path of his duty: but we tempt him to depart from his duty. Our strength is tried by frequent experiences; we are tempted by the weakness of our principles to give way to the violence of our passions.

We are allured by the appearances of things; we are tempted by the words of persons as well as the appearances of things; we are enticed by persuasions; we are seduced or decoyed by the influence and false arts of others.

Illustrations from the Scriptures

James chapter 1 deals with the dangers of misrepresentation. One such being the difference between trials and temptations. Verses 2 to 4 deal with temptations. Such come from within, and are to be resisted. When under temptation, we cannot excuse ourselves and say that such proceed from God. They come from within man; the process is from passion, through sin to death. The temptation of the Lord Jesus Christ in the wilderness (Matthew chapter 4) does not record the ravings of some lunatic when Satan addresses the Lord, but the claim of a disputed right. Satan considered that he was the firstborn, hence his claims. He even used Scripture, but the Lord answered; 'It is written **AGAIN**'. It is not the Scriptures Satan quoted here, but the parts of the Scriptures that he **omitted**. Compare Matthew 4:6 and the quote in Psalm 91:11 and 12. Satan does **not** continue and quote verse 13 because that verse concerns him!

Beware of the wiles of the devil.

Tidings

First mention
Genesis 29:13 'And it came to pass, when Laban heard the **tidings** of Jacob his sister's son, that he ran to meet him, and embraced him, and kissed him, and brought him to his house. And he told Laban all these things'.
Please note the result of hearing the tidings. So should the preaching of the Gospel bring its results, when the good tidings go out. 'And he told Laban **all** these things'. We must declare the whole counsel of God. Consider the effect when we hear the news on radio. Unless we have **all** the facts, how can we form an accurate opinion. So much these days is censored and edited out. This must **not** be so with the preaching of the gospel. The whole story must be told!

Synonyms
News implies anything that is new or anything that has not been heard before. It also includes that which may be known by others, but not by the person listening. It is therefore important when preaching the Gospel that we assume that the people have not heard before the message that we preach.

Tidings from the word tide, signifies that which flows in periodically like the tide. News is often unexpected. Tidings are expected. In time of war the public are eager after news: and they who have relatives in the armed forces, are anxious to have tidings of them.

Illustrations from the Scriptures
2 Timothy 4 verses 1 to 5 give us the responsibility that we must bare in preaching the gospel. We must preach

the Word. We must keep to the facts. We must keep to the Scriptures. We must not paraphrase the Scriptures. For instance: to declare that Christ was punished for our sins is not a scriptural phrase. Keep to the Scriptures and explain them.

Remember it is simple to be difficult but... it is difficult to be simple.

Transgression

First mention
Exodus 23:21 'Beware of him, and obey his voice, provoke him not; for he will not pardon your **transgressions**: for my name is in him'.

The word is closely linked with obeying the voice of God, keeping His commandments, and the necessity for pardon when His commands are disobeyed.

Synonyms
Offence is a general term, signifying the act that offends. Trespass is contracted from *trans* and *pass* and signifies a passing beyond. Transgress has its root in Latin and signifies a going beyond. The offence, therefore, which constitutes a trespass, arises out of the law of property. A passing over or treading upon the property of another is a trespass. The offence which constitutes a transgression, flows out of the laws of society in general which fix the boundaries of right and wrong. Whoever, therefore, goes beyond or breaks these bounds is guilty of a transgression. The Trespass is a species of offence which peculiarly applies to the land or premises of

individuals: transgression is a species of moral as well as political evil.

An offence is either public or private. A misdemeanour is properly a private offence, and signifies an offence in one's demeanour against propriety. A misdeed is always private, and it signifies a wrong deed, or a deed which offends against one's duty.

An offence is that which affects persons or principles, communities or individuals, and is committed either directly or indirectly against the person. An affront is altogether personal, and is directly brought to bear against the front of some particular person. Offences are either against God or man; a trespass is also an offence against God or man; a transgression is an offence against the will of God, as the verse in Exodus 23:21 shows. The misdemeanour is an offence against the established order of society; a misdeed is an offence against the law of God: and affront is an offence against good manners.

Illustrations from the Scriptures

Romans 4:15 links transgression with law, in stating that where there is no law there is no transgression. Sin was in the world from the very beginning, but the advent of the law turned the sinner into a transgressor.

1 John 3:4 defines sin in terms of transgression by stating that sin is the transgression of the law, taking us back to the narrative of Genesis chapter 3.

Trespass

First mention
Genesis 31:36 'And Jacob was wroth, and chode with Laban: and Jacob answered and said to Laban, What is my **trespass**? what is my sin, that thou hast so hotly pursued after me?'

The word is inseparably linked with sin, and being pursued with respect to that which had apparently been stolen.

Synonyms
Much of the ground has already been covered under the heading 'transgression', but a summary will be given here.

Trespass is contracted from *trans* and *pass* and signifies a passing beyond, whilst transgress has its root in Latin and signifies a going beyond. A trespass is an offence arising out of the law of property, whilst transgression is an offence against the laws that fix the right and the wrong.

Hunters are apt to commit trespass in the eagerness of their pursuit: the passions of men are perpetually misleading them and causing them to commit various transgressions.

We trespass upon the time or patience of another: we transgress the moral or civil law, and in particular, the law of God.

Illustrations from the Scriptures
Ephesians 2:1 links trespass with sins in which we found ourselves spiritually dead. Thus is the effect of

trespasses and sins, i.e. to bring about alienation from God, or in other words, spiritual death.

Colossians 2:13 speaks of the forgiveness of God for our trespasses, explained in the succeeding verse in its reference to the cross and the cancellation of the debt incurred.

Trial

First mention

Job 9:23 'If the scourge slay suddenly, he will laugh at the **trial** of the innocent'.

Note that the word is linked with the innocent, and therefore we conclude that the innocent do not escape the trials of life, Job being a case in point here. No moral order exists in the world, and God connives at injustice and laughs at its victims. Though we cannot deny that many comparatively innocent people perish, by what is sometimes described as 'an act of God', such as an earthquake or tempest, we can deny that Job is right in ascribing man's wickedness to God.

Synonyms

The word has already been equated with the word 'temptation', and here is a brief summary:

Trial is derived from the Hebrew to stretch, and signifies to stretch the power.

Tempt is derived from the Latin to stretch, and signifies to impel to action by efforts.

We try a person only in the path of his duty: but we tempt him to depart from his duty. Experience is derived from the Latin tongue and denotes to bring forth, that is, the thing brought to light, or the act of bringing to light.

Proof is derived from the Latin vocabulary and signifies to make good, or the thing made good.

Experience is that which has been tried: an experiment is the thing to be tried. Experience is certain, as it is a deduction from the past for the service of the present: the experiment is uncertain, and serves a future purpose. Experience is an unerring guide, which no man can desert without falling into error (for we even learn by our mistakes—and there are many examples of this in the Scriptures). Experience serves to lead us to moral truth: we profit by experience to rectify practice.

Trials are of absolute necessity in directing our conduct, and our way of life. The proof determines the judgment: so, in the knowledge of men and things, the proof of men's characters and merits is best made by observing their conduct.

Illustrations from the Scriptures

1 Peter 1:7 talks of the trial of our faith. So Peter had learnt his lessons well at the feet of the Lord, realising that it must be the suffering first, and the glory to follow. If we confess that we have faith, then we must be prepared to have that faith put to the test and proved—it will enrich our spiritual experience.

Trust

First mention

Deuteronomy 28:52 'And he shall besiege thee in all thy gates, until thy high and fenced walls come down, wherein thou **trustedst**, throughout all thy land: and he shall besiege thee in all thy gates throughout all thy land, which the LORD thy God hath given thee'.

The word, here, implies knowledge, familiarity, and reliance, and also suggests hope. The high walls were a prominence with which the people were familiar and relied upon for their salvation.

Synonyms

Part of the ground has already been covered under the heading of 'faith', a word with which it is often confused.

Trust, etymologically, is linked with hope. A person cannot be trusted until that person is known. Our faith in Christ at our salvation, did not imply that we knew Him: on the contrary, we were like the healed blind man of John 9 who knew nothing except that he could see. We learn to trust the Lord as we get to know Him over the years of our spiritual experience.

> 'Jesus, Jesus I am resting in the joy of what Thou art:
> I am finding out the greatness of Thy loving heart'.

We believe that Christ died for our sins: we trust Him day by day for protection.

Trust and confidence agree with hope in regard to the objects anticipated; they agree with expectation in regard to the certainty of the anticipation. Expectation, trust, and confidence, when applied to some future good, differ principally in the grounds on which the certainty or positive conviction rests. Expectation springs either from the character of the individual or the nature of the event which is the subject of anticipation.

Trust springs altogether from a view of the circumstances connected with the event, and is an inference or conclusion of the mind drawn from the whole. Confidence arises more from the temper of the mind than from the nature of the object.

Thus we expect our friends to assist us in time of need; we trust that an eminent physician will cure us—it is founded upon our knowledge of his skill.

Illustrations from the Scriptures

Both 2 John 12 and 3 John 14 use the word in the sense of hope, in his longing to see them once again.

Mark 10:24 uses the word in the sense of reliance when talking about the riches of this world.

1 Timothy 4:10 implies an experimental knowledge of God thereby being able to trust in God. We trust in the living God already knowing that He is our Saviour, having believed in Him.

Truth

First mention

Genesis 24:27 'And he said, blessed be the LORD God of my master Abraham, who hath not left destitute my master of His mercy and His **truth**; I being in the way, the LORD led me to the house of my master's brethren'.

The use of the word here implies that a person would be destitute if he did not have the truth of God. Therefore the truth of God enriches the soul. Mercy and truth are on a common platform here—they both enrich the soul, and they both have their source in God. Mercy is holding back from us that which we deserve: truth is giving to us that which we need.

Synonyms

Truth belongs to the thing: veracity to the person. The truth of the story is admitted upon the veracity of the narrator.

Fact is that part of the truth that represents a reality, or the real state of things.

Truth is said to be authentic when it is in accordance with fact.

Accuracy is that part of truth that has to do with correctness and exactness.

'Truth alone wounds'—Napoleon.

'Truth and fidelity are the pillars of the temple of the world; when these are broken, the fabric falls, and crushes all to pieces'—Felltham.

'Truth contradicts our nature, error does not, and for a very simple reason; truth requires us to regard ourselves as limited; error flatters us to think of ourselves as in one or other way unlimited'—Goethe.

'Truth does not conform itself to us, but we must conform ourselves to it'—M. Claudius.

'In this world, truth is for ever on the scaffold, wrong for ever on the throne'—Lowell.

'Truth is too simple for us; we do not like those who unmask our illusions'—Emerson.

'Truth is simple indeed, but we have generally no small trouble in learning to apply it to any practical purpose'—Goethe.

'Truths are first clouds, then rain, then harvests and food'—Ward Beecher.

Illustrations from the Scriptures

'What is truth?' asked Pilate of the Lord Jesus Christ. No verbal answer was necessary. Truth was standing before him. Over and above that which has already been said, truth is a Person—it is Christ (John 14:6). He is the embodiment of truth, and He spoke the truth at all times. Truth is more than a virtue—it is a way of life. John, in his epistles, speaks more of truth than the other writers. He, alone, was standing at the cross, not forsaking His Lord as the others. And thus at this place he learnt what truth was.

Let us go back to the cross and rediscover truth.

Ungodliness

First mention

2 Samuel 22:5 'When the waves of death compassed me, the floods of **ungodly** men made me afraid'.

The word is used in connection with enemies, with overwhelming numbers, together with the distresses of life. This awareness of the presence of the ungodly encourages the Psalmist to call upon the name of the Lord'.

Synonyms

Ungodly, like irreligious and impious, express what a person is not; profane expresses what a person is.

Ungodly implies neglecting God; irreligious implies neglecting religious things:

impious also implies neglecting such spiritual matters, but expresses a positive contempt for it.

Profane also implies a positive contempt for spiritual things. What a believer holds in reverence, and utters with awe, is pronounced with an air of indifference or levity, and as a matter of common discourse, by a profane man.

When we speak of a profane sentiment, or a profane joke, profane lips, and the like, the sense is personal and reproachful; impious is never implied but to what is personal, and in the very worst sense.

'I fear God, and next to God, I chiefly fear him who fears Him not'—Saadi.

Illustrations from the Scriptures

Romans 1:18 looks at ungodliness in the light of the wrath of God, and His righteousness. It is also equated with the unrighteousness of man, and the entire verse constitutes the charge laid against man in the high court of God.

Unity

First mention

Psalm 133:1 'Behold, how good and how pleasant it is for brethren to dwell in **unity**!'

Unity is equated with that which is good and pleasant and therefore desirable. It is not something that is spasmodic, but the word 'dwell' suggests a permanent state.

Synonyms

Add signifies to put to an object, and is derived from the Latin.

Join, originally from the Greek, signifies to bring into close contact.

Unite, from the Latin, signifies to make into one.

Coalesce, from the Latin, signifies to grow or form one's self together.

Uniformity, from the Latin, simply indicates one form.

Unity, as we know it in the Scriptures, is not uniformity or coalition.

Uniformity is said of things only as to their fitness to correspond.

Things coalesce by coming into an entire cohesion of all their parts.

Addition is opposed to subtraction: union to division: colation to distinction: uniformity to diversity.

Adding is either corporeal or spiritual action; joining is mostly said of corporeal objects; uniting is employed of spiritual things.

We add a wing to a house by a mechanical process, or we add quantities together by calculation; we join two armies together by placing them on the same spot; people are united who are bound to each other by similarity of opinions and belief.

'Unity, agreement, is always silent or soft voiced; it is only discord that loudly proclaims itself'—Carlyle.

Illustrations from the Scriptures

Ephesians 4:3 speaks of the unity of the Spirit, NOT the spirit of unity. The Holy Spirit unites—anything that divides or causes splits in assemblies cannot be of the Spirit of God. The unity of the Spirit is equated with the bond of peace.

There is one Lord
> one faith
> one baptism
> one Body
> one Spirit
> one hope
> one God.

There is absolute unity with God and we have to enter into the realisation of this.

Victory

First mention

2 Samuel 19:2 'And the **victory** that day was turned into mourning unto all the people: for the people heard say that day how the king was grieved for his son'.

Here was victory, but David was not entering into the realisation of it in the light of the death of his son. We have, and share in; the victory which Christ has won at the cross, but how often do we fail to realise it.

Synonyms

Conquer, from the Latin, signifies to seek or try to gain an object.

Subdue, from the Latin, signifies to give or put under.

Overcome signifies to come over or get the mastery over one.

Persons or things are conquered or subdued: persons only are vanquished. An enemy or a country is conquered; a foe is vanquished: people are subdued.

We conquer an enemy by whatever means we gain the mastery over him; we vanquish him, when by force we make him yield; we subdue him by whatever means we check or destroy in him the spirit of resistance.

A believer tries to conquer his enemies by kindness and generosity; a warrior tries to vanquish them in the field; a prudent monarch tries to subdue his rebellious subjects by a due mixture of clemency or rigor.

William the First conquered England by vanquishing his rival Harold: after which he completely subdued the English.

Whoever aims at maturity in the spiritual life must strive through the means of the power of the Holy Spirit of God to conquer avarice, pride, and every inordinate propensity; to subdue wrath, anger, lust and every carnal appetite; to overcome temptation, and to surmount trials and impediments which obstruct his course.

Illustrations from the Scriptures

When we think of victory, we cannot but help turn to 1 Corinthians 15 verse 55 and 57, where the grave has resigned its victory, and our victory is through our Lord Jesus Christ. This is set in contrast to the aspirations of the eager man of this world, as recorded in Ecclesiastes 9:11, which vividly describes the uncertainties of this life, and its unannounced catastrophes.

Vision

First mention

Genesis 15:1 'After these things the word of the LORD came unto Abram in a **vision**, saying, Fear not, Abram:

VISION

I am thy shield, and thy exceeding great reward'.

Please note a very important point here; the vision is closely connected with the word of the Lord. The vision, therefore, is of God's doing, and not of man's.

Synonyms

Vision, from the Latin, signifies either the act of seeing or the thing seen.

Apparition, from appear, signifies the thing that appears.

Phantom, from the Greek, is used for a false apparition, or the appearance of a thing otherwise than what it is.

Illustrations from the Scriptures

There are a triology of prophetic books that have much to do with visions, and will repay most careful study on the subject:

Ezekiel — visions of God
Daniel — visions of world kingdoms
Obadiah — visions of man's evil.

In Daniel, ch.2 and ch.7 run in parallel, and see the kingdoms of this world from different viewpoints:

Chapter 2 from man's standpoint (as an imposing figure of a man).

Chapter 7 from God's standpoint (as rapacious animals).

Many references to visions could be listed here, but here are some of the most significant:

To Abraham in various references in Genesis
To Jacob in Genesis 28:12
To Moses in Exodus 3:2
To Balaam in Numbers 22:31
To Joshua in Joshua 5:13

To Gideon in Judges 6:12
To Daniel as already mentioned
To Joseph in Matthew chapter 1.

Sometimes the vision was by an angel, in a human form, in a dream, or an object, such as the burning bush. In each case there was no doubt that God had spoken.

Voice

First mention
Genesis 3:8 'And they heard the **voice** of the LORD God walking in the garden in the cool of the day: and Adam and his wife hid themselves from the presence of the LORD God amongst the trees of the garden'.

Notice how God speaks, even though Adam and his wife had sinned, and the guilt of that sin was in evidence. It was a voice that spoke in the garden of Eden in the cool of the day. God came in peace, and spoke in peace.

Synonyms
Cry denotes a sound from the mouth, but voice indicates an utterance, an expression, an expressed opinion, one who speaks.

Noise is an inarticulate sound: voice is an articulate sound that can be understood by the listener.

Illustrations from the Scriptures
In Acts 9 and the conversion of Saul of Tarsus, the vision and the voice are closely linked. Both were for Saul, and for Saul alone. His companions heard some

kind of a voice, they saw no man, and consequently stood speechless.

The voice of God is described as thunder by the Psalmist. It came from heaven at the baptism of Jesus in Matthew 3:17. It was heard on the mount of transfiguration in Matthew 17:5

The voice of God is for those who will hear. God is always speaking: it is we who are not always hearing.

In John 1 there is a contrast between the Word of God and the voice in the wilderness. There may be a word with no voice, but there can never be a voice without a word.

Washing

First mention
Genesis 18:4 'Let a little water, I pray you, be fetched, and **wash** your feet, and rest yourselves under the tree'.
This first mention of washing is connected with water and the removal of defilement. It may seem obvious to connect washing with water, but it will be shown later on that this is most important.

Synonyms
Wash, cleanse, purify, and purge are all allied words, and can easily be confused with each other. It is well to keep to the words of Scripture when using such words. Hymn writers have tended to employ some poetic license over the years, and can leave a false impression. Wash denotes to make clean through the medium of

water. Some hymns use the word in relation to blood, yet its immediate link is with water as we shall see.

Cleanse is a stronger word and denotes to be rid of dirt, stain or whatever defiles. It is this word that is so closely connected with the blood of Christ as we shall see.

Purify is a yet stronger word that signifies to make pure in the sense of carrying off whatever is impure or superfluous, as the dross from molten metal.

Illustrations from the Scriptures

Ephesians 5:26 declares that the sanctification and cleansing of the church is with the washing by the Word. Note now washing is connected with water, the latter being a symbol of not only the Spirit, but the Word.

Titus 3:5 speaks of the washing of regeneration. This reference takes us back to John 3 and the interview with Nicodemus, where we read of being born of water and of the Spirit. Baptismal regeneration, as an interpretation, would be foreign to the teaching of the Word of God, whilst to say that baptism itself is in mind here, would be nothing less than a glaring anachronism. The water suggests the Word of God (1 Peter 1:23).

Revelation 1:5 refers to being washed from our sins in His own blood. There is only one letter difference in the Greek between the verb 'washed' and 'loosed'. As washing with blood is wholly unknown to the law in the Old Testament, it seems that the word here would be better translated 'loosed'.

Psalm 51:7 can only be explained by going backwards to the law of the leper in his day of cleansing. First there was the sprinkling of the blood of the bird, then he that is cleansed shall wash his clothes and wash himself in water that he may be clean. And after that—and only after—shall he come into the camp.

Will of God

First mention
Ezra 7:18 'And whatsoever shall seem good to thee, and to thy brethren, to do with the rest of the silver and the gold, that do after the **will of your God**'.

This is a remarkable verse that forms part of a letter to Ezra from king Artaxerxes, as Ezra returns to Jerusalem to rebuild. That a man of the world should speak in terms of the will of God, throws much light upon the meaning of the will of God, coupled with His sovereignty. The reality is that many people of this world will one day discover that in all their dealings, they have performed the will of God. How much more should the child of God do the will of God out of a loving heart.

Synonyms
The will is that faculty of the soul which is the most prompt and decisive; it immediately impels to action.

The wish is but a gentle motion of the soul towards a thing.

The will must be under the entire control of God, or it will lead a soul into mischief.

Wishes must be under the control of the will of God, or otherwise they may greatly disturb our spiritual balance.

The three truths, the will of God, the sovereignty of God, and the guidance of God are closely allied.

The sovereignty of God implies that God **MUST** have His own way (q.v. Romans 9).

The will of God implies that God's way can be performed through the believer's life.

The guidance of God is that continuing spiritual exercise whereby the believer might know the will of God in his life.

Illustrations from the Scriptures

See the separate treatise, dealing with the subject under the heading of four questions.

The Will of God

References: Matt. 6:10; 11:28-30; 21:28-31; Acts 16:10; Rom. 12:1 and 2.

The subject comes under four headings:
1. **What is meant by the will of God?**
2. **Why should I do the will of God?**
3. **How can I know the will of God?**
4. **How should I do the will of God?**

1. **What is meant by the will of God?** wish = a gentle motion towards a thing, but will = something prompt, decisive and demands action. q.v. Matt. 11:28-30. Yoke helps to pull a load, must fit correctly, must be the right yoke. Yoke of Christ = 'I am meek and lowly'. Meekness is NOT weakness but

THE WILL OF GOD

a source of strength = obedience and resignation to the will of God.

Will is NOT fate. Fate is too impersonal. Will of God is personal as we shall see.

a. **revealed will of God** i.e. as contained in Word of God re. unequal yoke, woman maintaining silence, our sanctification (1 Thess 4:3).

b. **concealed will of God** i.e. for the individual, for specific circumstances e.g. one's career, promotion, moving away, new house, new district, leaving assembly, marriage, the Lord's service, right message for a meeting. All these need heart searching and much prayer.

c. **active obedience** = obey Him and do His will.

d. **passive obedience** = submit to His will.

e. **knowing is not enough** like the winter sun—gives light but no heat. Knowing the will of God and NOT doing it makes the matter worse.

2. **Why should I do the will of God?**

   a. **God's prerogative** q.v. Rom. 9 and the sovereignty of God. He must have His way.

   b. **God's plan** q.v. Rom. 12:2 'good and acceptable and perfect will of God. Deut. 13:4 'The Lord commands—to keep His statutes'.

   c. **Man's proving** the mark of his sincerity. Rom 12:1 'present our bodies...'. Show our love to Christ by being willing to learn of Him, Matt. 11:28-30.

   d. **Man's profit** Deut. 10:13 'for thy good'. Brings benefit, blessing and peace.

   e. **Man's privilege** Our honour to serve Him and to do His will.

   f. **Man's purpose** to be like Christ q.v. John 6:38

'came not to do His own will...'. John 4:34. 'my meat—do the will of Him that sent me'. Is there a family likeness yet?

3. How can I know the will of God?

a. **Conviction** work of the Spirit. Arrow to the soul. No peace until resolved.

b. **Conclusion** q.v. Acts 16:10 'assuredly gathering' came to a conclusion. Spirit calls on their past experiences. God makes use of our intelligent co-operation.

c. **Circumstances** q.v. Acts 16:7 'forbidding' lit. to cause to have an accident (from Greek). Sometimes the Lord lays afflictions upon us to steer us in the right direction. q.v. experiences of Ruth, Noami, Job, David and Paul's thorn in the flesh.

d. **Communion** by prayer in the Spirit, q.v. Luke 11 taught them what to pray for, NOT how to pray. God does NOT give useless or harmful things. Come boldly to Him Luke 11:13 pray for the Spirit i.e. the operation and the influence of the Spirit. Need for spiritual discernment and perception here.

e. **Continuity** ONE STEP AT A TIME, q.v. Ps 119:105, 'Thy word is a lamp unto my feet'.

4. How should I do the will of God?

q.v. Matt. 6:10 'in the earth as it IS in heaven'.

a. **by expedience** q.v. Acts 4:19 'hearken unto you more than God?'

b. **by example**

regularly q.v. offerings in Leviticus.

entirely Num. 15:40 'do ALL my commandments'.

sincerely Gen. 22 offering of Isaac—contrary to flesh and blood.

willingly 1 Chron. 28:9 Solomon 'serve the Lord with willing mind'.

fervently Rom. 12:11 'fervent in Spirit, serving the Lord'.

wholeheartedly Num. 18:29 'out of all your gifts, ye shall offer all the best', q.v. offerings in Lev. The fat is the Lord's.

Readily and swiftly Dan. 9:21 Gabriel caused to fly swiftly.

Constantly Rev. 7:15 serve Him day and night. Ps. 106:3 'doeth righteousness at all times'.

The ultimate ambition to know God's will and to do it before being asked.

Works

First mention
Exodus 5:4 'And the king of Egypt said unto them, Wherefore do ye, Moses and Aaron, let the people from their **works**? get you unto your burdens'.

The context shows that the children of Israel were under bondage, in Egypt, to the king, and their works, no matter how great they were, would never deliver them from the bondage of Egypt. That deliverance was to be by blood and then by power. So it is today: no works, no matter how great, can save from the bondage of this world. Redemption is by blood and by power—God has not changed.

Synonyms
Work is the general term, as including that which calls

for the exertion of our strength: labour differs from it in the degree of exertion required. Toil expresses a still higher degree of painful exertion: drudgery implies a mean and degrading work.

A man wishes to complete his work; he is desirous of resting from his labour; he seeks respite from his toil; he submits to drudgery.

Illustrations from the Scriptures

The parable of the Pharisee and the Publican in Luke 18 serves to show how works will not save. The Pharisee came to be seen; the Publican came to be heard. The Pharisee came to give; the Publican came to receive. Ephesians 2:9 emphasises that salvation is not of works, lest any man should boast. Any gospel that by-passes the cross is no gospel at all. John 10 is not slow to tell us that the thief and the robber will endeavour to enter another way. Those that try to enter heaven another way, other than by the cross, are thieves and robbers.

Under the heading of 'justification' we have dealt with two apparently conflicting issues:

Justification by faith and Justification by works.

The former is dealt with in Romans chapters 3 and 4, whilst the latter is dealt with in James 2. The latter is the complement of justification by faith. The former has to do with God, the latter with man. Thus we are justified by our works (as believers) in the sight of man, for man can only judge from the outside. There is no conflict: justification owns grace and does homage to the blood.

World

First mention

1 Samuel 2:8 'He raiseth up the poor out of the dust, and lifteth up the beggar from the dunghill, to set them among princes, and to make them inherit the throne of glory: for the pillars of the earth are the LORD's, and He hath set the **world** upon them'.

This verse stresses God's supremacy over the world, and therefore His control over it. Salvation, here, is expressed in terms of being raised out of the dust of this world, and being lifted up from its dunghill.

Synonyms

Cosmos, derived directly from the Greek, implies an order and arrangement. In Scripture it signifies that order as governed by Satan, complete with its politics, rivalry, and pride. Outwardly it appears to be cultured and religious, but underneath this veneer, it is seething with national and international rivalry. In a time of crisis, modern civilisation can only uphold itself by military might.

Earth, another term used, implies the terrestrial ball upon which we live, and all the minerals it contains. Psalm 24:1 'The earth is the LORD's, and the fulness thereof'.

The word 'age' or 'generation' denotes a period of time, when we talk about 'the man of the world', implying a man of his times, or generation.

The term 'people' can also be considered to be the world, in the sense of the inhabited world.

Worldly signifies after the manner of this world.

Secular signifies belonging to time or this life.
Temporal signifies lasting only for time.

Illustrations from the Scriptures

Quite a remarkable phrase appears in 1 John 2:15: 'love not the world'. The word for 'love' is the same word as used for the love of God in the Greek manuscripts. God gave everything. Do not give everything to the world.

Romans 12:2 exhorts us not to be conformed to this world. This refers to the fleeting fashions of this world, and being squeezed into a mold, or pattern, according to the manner of this world.

James deals with many dangers, and chapter 4 deals with the dangers of worldliness thus:

1. **Rivalry** verse 1 to 3
   Method and Motive.
2. **Infidelity** verse 4 and 5
   Enmity and Envy.
3. **Pride** verses 6 and 7
   God resists the proud and assists the humble.
4. **Corruption** verse 8
   Hands and Heart.
5. **Success** verses 9 and 10
   Good times and Greatness.
6. **Slander** verse 11
   No respect and no recognition.
7. **Criticism** verse 12
   Assertion and Assumption.
8. **Boasting** verses 13 and 14
   Unthinking and Uncertainty.
9. **Godlessness** verse 15
   Self made and self sufficient.
10. **Evil** verse 16 and 17
    Over confident and overlooking.

Worship

First mention

Genesis 22:5 'And Abraham said unto his young men, Abide ye here with the ass; and I and the lad will go yonder and **worship**, and come again to you'.

This first mention of worship implies obedience and sacrifice. Obedience to the will of God, and to worship in the manner prescribed by God; and sacrifice in the sense of giving everything—'thine only Isaac'.

Synonyms

Adore, derived from the Latin, has in its meaning to pray to.

Worship, derived from the Saxon worthship, implies either the object that is worth, or the worth itself.

Adoration is the service of the heart towards God, in which we acknowledge our dependance and obedience, by petition and thanksgiving.

Worship consists in the outward form of showing reverence to God.

Adoration is the service of the heart towards God, in which we acknowledge our dependance and obedience, by petition and thanksgiving.

Worship consists in the outward form of showing reverence to God.

Adoration can with propriety be paid only to the one true God; worship can be offered by heathens to sticks and stones.

We adore God at all times and in all places, whenever the heart is lifted up towards Him.

We worship Him only at stated times, and according to the commands that God has laid down.

We seldom adore without worshipping: but we too frequently worship without adoring.

To the world, the act of worship implies emulating one's idol, in the sense of speaking, walking, dressing, and behaving like that object of worship. If we claim to worship God, then it behoves us to be in all points like Him.

Worship also embraces the following terms:

Devotion	—implying addiction and loyalty (q.v. 1 Corinthians 16:15).
Homage	—implying acknowledgement of the supremacy of God.
Service	—that which can only follow true worship.
Prayer	—implying not only our needs, but holy conversation with God.
Thanksgiving	—an expression of gratitude for all that God has wrought in us and for us.
Praise	—to commend the merits of, to glorify and extol the attributes of God.
Glorification	—to exalt and make great the name of our God.

Illustrations from the Scriptures

There are several references that indicate the way that we should worship:

Genesis 22:5 as already stated, requires implicit obedience.

Exodus 34:14 states that we should worship no other God.

Wrath

1 Chronicles 16:20 declares that we should worship in the beauty of holiness.
John 4:23 tells us to worship the Father in Spirit.

Wrath

First mention
Genesis 39:19 'And it came to pass, when his master heard the words of his wife, which she spake unto him, saying, After this manner did thy servant to me; that his **wrath** was kindled'.

Although this reference is not concerned with the wrath of God, but rather the wrath of man, it nevertheless yields an important clue to the meaning of the word. The wrath was kindled, suggesting that it was not there before this incident. The occasion that provoked the officer was the alleged invasion into that which was rightfully his own.

Synonyms
Anger, derived from the Latin, meaning vexation, implies acting against from its root meaning.
Resentment, derived from the French, signifies to feel again, over and over.
Wrath, derived from the Saxon, signifies heat or anger.
Ire, derived from the Latin, means the same as wrath.
Indignation, derived from the Latin, marks the strong feeling which base conduct awakens in the mind.
Resentment is less vivid than anger, and anger than wrath, ire or indignation. Anger is a sudden sentiment

of displeasure; resentment is a continued anger; wrath is a heightened sentiment of anger, which is poetically expressed by the word ire.

Anger may be either a selfish or a disinterested passion; it may be provoked by injuries done to others. In this latter sense of strong displeasure, God is angry with those who will not repent after many pleadings of God through His servants.

Wrath and ire are the sentiments of a superior towards an inferior. The wrath of God may be provoked by the persevering impenitence of sinners.

Indignation is a sentiment awakened by the unworthy and atrocious conduct of others.

A warmth of constitution sometimes gives rise to sallies of anger; depravity of heart breeds resentment; but indignation can flow from a high sense of honour and virtue.

Illustrations from the Scriptures

Romans 1:18, in stating the charge against man in God's high court, explains that the wrath of God is revealed from heaven against all ungodliness and unrighteousness of men, who hold, or suppress the truth in unrighteousness.

The book of Revelation give us a taste of the seven vials full of the wrath of God. Revelation 6:16 describes it in a most vivid way, when John speaks of the wrath of the Lamb. An apparent contradiction in terms, yet a stark reality, as this world is yet to experience.

In the light of the coming day of wrath (Revelation 6:17) it behoves us to teach and preach the Gospel faithfully, and to ensure in these days of ignorance, that the people understand clearly.